IF I HAD KNOWN

*The Truth about Unforgiveness and Key
Lessons You Should Know*

Pamela Simwanza

IF I HAD KNOWN: *The Truth about Unforgiveness and Key Lessons You Should Know*

Cover design by Pamela Simwanza
Credits: Kstudio-Feepik
Copyrights © 2019 Pamela Simwanza

Printed in the United Kingdom
Published by Amazon
ISBN: 9781097309894

This book recounts events in the life of Pamela Simwanza according to the author's recollection and perspective. Whilst all the stories are true, names and identities have been anonymised to protect the privacy of those involved.

CONTENTS

LESSONS LEARNT

EXTRAS

ACKNOWLEDEGEMTS

Jimmy, my biggest fan, my counsellor, my precious husband. Remember when I said to you, I think it's time to write a book. Your response was, 'finally! It's about time!' I said to you that I would write it and print only three copies one for you, myself and our future children but you questioned it. You made me realise that my testimony can bless many more people. You said, 'if the point isn't to share it with the world and for people to see God's goodness, then is there a point in writing it at all?' Not only are you my fan and counsellor, you are my teacher, friend and mentor. I appreciate the guidance you give me and the way you are with me. I have grown so much in my walk with God and I want to thank you. I respect you, I love you and every day with you has been a blessing. Thank you for supporting and encouraging my purpose.

Most importantly, my most sincere gratitude goes to God, the great leader in the ship of my life. You know my name, you know me. You knew my strengths before I discovered them. Thank you for not giving up on me. Thank you for gracing me daily and making me a part of your perfect plan. I am excited to see what surprises you have in store for me next, you never cease to amaze me. Thank you.

INTRODUCTION

Pain, resentment, emotional distress, confusion, isolation, judgement and a burdened heart, are just a few emotions I experienced towards a loved one, following on from an accusation that changed my life in an instant. Eight years later, I have reflected back on the events that took place in my life and I am now able to see things from another perspective. The journey to where I stand now, emotionally and spiritually, has not been easy. Many tears have been shed and distress caused. However, I wonder if all this emotional strain, or even half, could have been prevented if I understood the importance of forgiveness? Maybe, but then again maybe not. What hinders uncertainty, is things would have been different if "I HAD KNOWN".

This book has two sections; the first section talks about my personal story and has reflective accounts regarding revelations (about specific topics) I got whilst writing this book. The second, about four key lessons (with the use of research, theory and practical steps) that I want to raise awareness about and encourage readers to be mindful of, if like me, you dealt with or are still dealing with unforgiveness. Some of the feelings mentioned above, are a few reasons that give you every right to hold a grudge in your heart against someone. In your lifetime, someone you love and trust, might hurt you in a way that may be hard to process or understand. You might find it difficult to trust again, believe again or even love again. I have experienced such anguish but have also experienced freedom.

I've learnt a lot during my testing time. As a result, I have made a vow to always forgive others no matter what, as I now understand that forgiveness is for my benefit. In fact, I will go as far as saying that forgiveness is a selfish act because its purpose is solely for the wellbeing of the person offended. As much as I would love for you to share my view that forgiveness is for the benefit of the person who has been offended, I know that it may require more substance for you to share this view with me. For this reason, let us start from the beginning of my story.

IF I HAD KNOWN

CHAPTER 1

A Carefree Life

Recapping from what I was told, I was left in the care of my great-grandma at the age of six months, so my mother could migrate to the UK, to join my father. I, soon after, moved to Suhum (Ghana) to live with my grandma as the living conditions at my great-grandma's place were not suitable to bring up a child in. Although I lived in grandma's house, my great- grandma looked after me. We laughed together, she hid hot chocolate under her bed for me when I was hungry (late at night) and would wrap digestive biscuits in newspaper for me to take to school (additional to what grandma had already given me).

I don't remember a lot, but I remember having birthday celebrations every year, which I was told, mum funded. I remember getting lots of clothes, shoes and toys which I was told were from mum. I remember hearing regularly, 'one day you will see her, and she will come for you'. I didn't have to know mum physically to be fond of her. She was my superhero because, although we didn't see each other, she was prevalent in many areas of my life.

Grandma had a huge compound house. She had the main house which consisted of five rooms, where myself, my cousins, great-grandma and the house help lived. The other house was the 'boys' quarters' which consisted of four rooms. Various people moved in and out of 'the boys' quarters' as the years went past, some of them worked for her and others, were working professionals renting a place.

Grandma was a no-nonsense type of woman and although very strict, she had a good heart. She took in young people (and some extended family members) without family/ living in poorer conditions, brought them into her home and looked after them. Sometimes, they stayed for many years and other times, for a short while. They worked for her (housekeeping, house maintenance, gardening, hard labourer etc) in exchange for her care (meeting their basic health and care needs).

Grandma was very popular and respected in the town we lived in. Everybody knew her, maybe because she was the local midwife or the only person who owned a pharmacy, in the entire town later in her life.

I had a fun carefree childhood whilst growing up, from running through the mechanic grounds next to our house to planting vegetables and eating cocoa from the cocoa tree in our back garden. Sundays were good days for me. Aside from going to church in my best outfit, I knew that when we got home, we would be having coconut which gave me something to look forward to. My life as a child growing up in Suhum wasn't too bad, even with the corporal punishments experienced from school and from my grandmother.

I was a very popular, active, smart and witty child. Most people knew me around our neighbourhood and the same likability followed me throughout my school years. I went to a private school about a half hour walk away from our house. I don't remember much about being in nursery, but I remember always getting awards and recognition from teachers. Primary school was the same sort of experience, I had a lot of friends and was somewhat of a teacher's pet. My school was very diverse and had children from all over the world attending there.

My French teacher (originally from France) ordered that we speak French every Thursday (maybe this contributed to me getting a C in GCSE French, although I cannot understand a word of French to date) and the school ordered that we speak English on the other days. My French teacher was very fascinating, he was very tall and skinny with pale white skin. When it came to punishment, he seemed somewhat clueless in the caning department. Being caned by him was unpredictable, the cane would hit nearly every part of the body which I believe, confused him as it did his students, much like striking a nail with an unskilled hammersmith.

I remember my science teacher being very strict and unpopular amongst students. Often when he punished through caning, the accuracy, malice and aggression left us in keeled over pain. I remember a specific incident in which he caned me soo hard, it left me bleeding. Although very painful, it was a blessing in disguise as grandma stormed into school and ordered that no teacher ever hit me again.

My Religious Education (R.E) teacher, who I believe played a significant role in my Christian life to date was different. Although I went to church religiously on Sundays, my R.E teacher's influence is what pushed me to have some supernatural encounters with God through visions and dreams whilst growing up. My R.E teacher had a close relationship with God, and this was evident in the way he was with his students. He took a few students under his wing (including me) and mentored us. I remember visiting his home with some friends to pray and discuss the word of God additional to the prayers during school times.

School in Suhum, for me was enjoyable, there was a lot of banter in many of my classes especially towards the nineteen-year-old boy and girl in the same class as us 11-year olds. We often teased them about the fact that they should have been further ahead in their education and our seniors but just like many countries in Africa, academic progress is measured by intelligence not age. Most children knew me as the child whose parents were in the UK and often questioned when I'd be joining them abroad.

If you have grown up in any other country outside of Europe, you will know that the UK and other European countries are held in high esteem. I was very excited to join my mum and dad, and to see the UK in the future due to how it was portrayed to me not only by friends at school but by society. I was told all types of stories by the children in my class who had never been to Europe. The funny thing is, if you haven't been to Europe you would believe anything!

Though my parents were not with me, this was not an uncommon experience. Several children in my school, like me, grew up with other family members, as their parent (s) were in the UK or America and like me, were looking forward to the day they finally met them. I was content with my life as a child and knew that I had a good standard of life. I lived in a beautiful home, I was well cared for and never lacked anything, unlike some of my friends. I knew I was lucky, and I was grateful for that.

My Reflective Account about Corporal Punishment

When I was growing up in Ghana, discipline in the form of corporal punishment or physical chastisement was common and certainly wasn't classified as abuse as it was an acceptable practice in the country. Myself, my cousins whom I grew up with, as well as my friends all experienced "discipline" regularly for various reasons. In my case, not knowing all my timetables or the answers to the question's teachers asked me, was one of the main reasons I got caned at school. At home, the punishments I received also varied, caning and the occasional hitting on my fingertips with a ruler (such a simple yet extremely painful experience) were some of the regulars.

In my opinion, all the corporal punishments were not necessary as it did not stop me from making mistakes but instead, made me fearful of the people whom I considered my guardians. A child should not be fearful of the people he/she considers as his/her caregiver. The excessive discipline made me anxious when my name was said out loud because I didn't know if I had done something wrong or not.

I became anxious when I made a mistake because I knew the consequences I would endure. I became fearful of making mistakes which is ironic because mistakes need to be made for learning to be gained. Looking back at my experiences and that of most people I grew up with both in Ghana and in the UK, it is evident that physical chastisement or corporal punishment is the most common form of discipline used within Black and Minority Ethnic (BME) communities.

Although, at times I and my friends made jokes about how we were "disciplined", behind the laughs were also embedded memories of the suffering and pains inflicted on us. Many BME families argue that, physical discipline or corporal punishment is the most efficient way of instilling obedience into children. Often, families from BME backgrounds use religious sayings such as "whoever spares the rod hates their children, but the one who loves their children is careful to discipline them" to justify their acts of abuse. Some people argue that, such practices are down to generational cultural traditions. Others claim that, such acts have a link to slavery where punishment, (often physical abuse and torture) was used as a response for disobedience.

Whilst the practice of physical chastisement or corporal punishment was not considered as abuse in Ghana (and many other countries) when I was growing up, some children and young people around me had experiences that left them with severe injuries, some requiring medical attention. It is evident that, physical chastisement causes pain to children but beyond that is psychological trauma if punishment is unreasonable. Hitting a child with a cane, a belt or any other implement for his/her wrongdoing, does not promote positive communication but rather violence. Other methods of discipline such as withholding privileges, grounding and time out are safer and effective. This allows a child to meditate on their actions leading to a change in behaviour. Explaining to a child why you have withdrawn privileges will not instil fear, but rather effective communication skills and a stimulating environment.

Discipline is an expectation of every parent or guardian as the purpose of it is to create an orderly, stable, healthy environment for a child (ren). However, positive discipline supports a change in behaviour and communicates good values.

CHAPTER 2

First Contact

I often walked home alone, with my cousin, or friends after school and this was my normal routine. One day, an uncle came to pick me up with another man whom I recognised but didn't know where from. After about 10 minutes into our walk, it dawned on me that the other man was my father, I recognised him from the photos my grandma had shown me of him. I was filled with excitement and couldn't believe that my father was with me. It was an emotional afternoon for the both of us. I jumped at him in attempts to give him a hug and from the tears lingering in his eyes I knew that he was feeling what I felt.

I left Suhum with dad and spent some time with him and his family in Accra, (the capital of Ghana) for a while. I had the opportunity to meet my paternal cousins and family for the first time. We had a lot of fun together, we went shopping, had ice cream, went out to eat and just enjoyed quality time together, before dad left for the UK. This was my very first memory with my dad; I met him for the first time, at the age of ten.

I met mum for the first time when I was eleven, approximately a year after I met dad. I don't remember the details of our meeting, but I remember being supported by a relative to another town in Ghana. I remember running into the house (where I was told she was in) in search for her, looking through various rooms and then, I remember finally seeing her in the bedroom.

I recognised mum instantly as she resembled the woman, I saw in the picture with the lime green dress who I thought looked so beautiful and elegant. We hugged each other so tightly, with tears dripping from both our faces, it was as though we were expressing a million thoughts in our silence. I can't describe the emotions I experienced then. I could only imagine that I would have felt overwhelmed and excited, to finally meet the woman I had seen in the pictures all my life.

I had a connection with mum straight away. I admired her and loved her dearly. I was overjoyed to meet the woman who gave birth to me, the woman I had heard so much about all my life. We spent a lot of time together, we went everywhere from restaurants, to shopping, to visiting old friends and family.

Mum had bought me some new clothes from the UK which I loved and looked good in, especially the cord set of white and red floral high neck cropped top and skirt. I knew I was really going to get on with mum when I finally had the opportunity to join her (in the UK) as we had a lot of fun together.

What made me sure of this was, when I lied about knowing how to cook all types of foods, when mum asked me if I knew how to cook. I lied only to impress her. I mean I could cook but not anything sophisticated, as I was only 11 at the time, but I nodded confidently as I didn't want to disappoint her. I decided to make corn beef stew that turned out to be more like a soup. Although, I knew the food was bad and was sure mum did too, her response to it was what made me come to the realisation that we would get on just fine. She praised me for it, told me it tasted nice and helped me out a little bit before eating it with me.

The sort of relationship I had built with mum, over that short period of time we spent together was so significant to me. Hence, why I was soo heartbroken when I found out that she was leaving again to return to the UK and without me. Mum promised to do everything she could to get me to join her, she had already started the process and was hoping that my application would be accepted.

Although, I didn't know anything about the process or application I believed mum and had faith, so we prayed together on our knees one of the few nights she had left, and this is when I had a vision.

In the vision, I saw a small book with a blue sticker on it, the sticker had numbers on it, and it was stuck to the back of the small burgundy book. I didn't recognise the book, but I knew in my heart that my application had been accepted. So, I told mum the vision I saw, and she explained that from what I had described to her what I saw was a passport. We were both overjoyed and declare amen in faith, to confirm that what I had seen would become a reality very soon.

CHAPTER 3

20th November

I was informed about the good news not long after mum left Ghana. I remember telling all my friends at school about it, which of course, came with their request list of what they wanted me to send them when I got to the UK.

When I migrated to the UK in November one of the first things, I noticed was the weather, I didn't understand why it was so cold. The sight of children and adults walking down the road with their hands tucked tightly away in their pockets whilst vapour came out of their nose and mouth with every breath, caused a chilling atmosphere throughout the entire street.

The UK looked nothing like how I had imagined it all those years, the houses were small and people were often tucked away in them, the community was not how it was like, in Ghana. I didn't see children running around unless I was at a park and I certainly couldn't get coconut on Sundays from the back garden. It wasn't as free as I imagined it would be, in fact, it wasn't as elegant as I thought it would be either. I quickly got accustomed to the fact that I was in a different environment and that my life was different, but I didn't mind this change as I was now with my mum, sisters and stepfather.

Prior to moving to the UK, I knew that my parents had separated and had both remarried with children, but I never thought much about it. I didn't question it as a child, even after I moved to the UK, but I guess it's because I didn't grow up with my parents, had never seen them together, so felt indifferent about it.

I started school and was shocked at how the students got away with disobedience and disrespect towards the teachers. Although I was already accustomed to the diversity at the school and was achieving above the expected standard academically, there were so many questions I had running through my mind concerning the student's mannerisms and the lack of power and authority the teachers and leaders had.

It didn't help that the school I was attending did not have a good reputation, but what shocked me the most was the fact that there was no discipline by the teachers. The students ruled everything, and this confused me. I was not use to this. I was not used to seeing children get away with throwing things and shouting back at their teachers. Although at this point, I had come to the realisation that there was a no caning or hitting policy, I didn't even consider stepping out of line due to the fear instilled in me from my previous experiences and the cultural principles I knew.

I quickly began to lose myself simply because I didn't fit in. The carefree, popular, active, smart and witty child running around Suhum was now replaced with a shy, lost, introverted child. I was no longer in my comfort zone and I was fully aware of it. My accent didn't sound like everyone else's and, I dressed to meet the standards of the school's policy and did everything I could to not draw any attention to myself.

I made friends with the students whom I knew had a similar story to mine, or like me, were not trying to draw attention to themselves. The reputation of the school is what caused mum to move me to another school. Even with this change, the same conduct I had in the previous school followed me. I found myself in a group of friends whom like me obeyed and followed the rules.

CHAPTER 4

The Absent Father

I remember mum driving up to dad's house, not long after I had arrived in the UK. He didn't know that I was here, as mum had always maintained that he did not contribute to me coming to the UK. In fact, I was told that he said to her "leave her, when she is older, she can find her way here like we all did". I am guessing, that is why he was surprised to see me outside his window, when I rang to let him know I was standing outside his house over a year after I saw him in Ghana. I spent some time with dad after I moved to the UK, his house was about a 10-minute drive away from where mum lived.

Dad always read the sun newspaper and would go to Gregg's to get me and my brothers some sausage rolls, when he had a late shift at work. I remember the radio and the white fluffy coat he bought me, I remember visiting dad's sister in Hackney and having dinner with her several times. I remember going to Tesco with dad and my brothers for small grocery shops without failure to pick up Sunny D every time.

Dad and mum had a good relationship although no longer together but at some point, this changed, and I still cannot pinpoint exactly when this happened or what happened.

We moved from London to Hampshire about three years after I moved to the UK following on from mum's relationship breakdown with my sister's father, this move meant that contact with dad was limited. In fact, so limited that I remember seeing him again when I was around 15 years old during a school holiday. Unfortunately, this contact with dad did not last for the whole week as intended, it ended after a couple of days due to an acrimony between mum and dad, about child support. I remember dad saying that his mother had just passed away leaving him financially unstable to support me at the time. Mum came to get me from his house, saying she will be taking him to child support as that was not an excuse to not support me financially.

Following on from that incident, I did not see dad for many years and the next time I saw him unexpectedly, was around Christmas time a few years later when mum and I were shopping in London. I remember seeing him and my brothers through a busy crowd. As we drew near to each other, he gave me a hug alongside my brother, and we had a chat about how things had been. It was emotional as there was a lot of things unsaid (I could feel it) but our encounter was short as I was with mum who had walked into a shop after seeing my father. The encounter replayed itself in my mind throughout the rest of my day in London due to the intense emotions I felt.

Throughout the years, I would often think about what life would be like if dad was around, I often had these thoughts when I hit milestones in my life i.e. starting college, getting awards, passing my driving lesson and graduating from university. A part of me wished he was around but a part of me was so angry at him due to the things I would hear mum say about her experience with him when they were together. She sometimes talked about the lack of his role in my life as a father often comparing it to the involvement my sister's father had in their lives although they were no longer together.

Slowly, I started to share the same views as my mum about my dad. The view that he doesn't take care of his responsibility or care about me. This view made sense to me as it was in line with the frequency of contact, I had with dad. The contact we had with each other was mainly over text messages here and there, coupled with occasional phone calls during birthdays and Christmases.

It was evident that my mother felt negatively about my father, her version of events about why their relationship ended was because he wasn't man enough and did not look out for her when his sister bullied her. Mum sometimes talked about making dad dinner when they lived together but her food was pushed aside and replaced with dad's sister's food and he never stuck up for her. I never really knew the full details of their relationship and didn't really question it either. However, I knew my mum was still hurt from whatever happened because of how she spoke about him and men in general. I felt her pain most when she was upset or we disagreed on something because I would hear things like "you are just like your father, you have book sense but no common sense".

Although I didn't know much about dad, he seemed like a nice man but a huge part of me was very angry with him for not being there for me and not taking care of his responsibility. This huge part of me (mostly influenced by mums' experiences) as well as other significant events I went through later in my life (where I felt that if he was around maybe things would have been different), all exacerbated my anger towards dad.

My Reflective Account about Absent Fathers

Now that I am older and can assess and understand situations, I cannot stress enough, how easily children growing up in single parent homes can be impacted. The absence of a parent whether physically or emotionally can influence the type of relationship a child has with the opposite sex. I felt obligated to side with mum automatically regarding her perceptions of men although I hadn't experienced the same relationships and traumas she had. She was my caregiver and the parent who showed consistency in meeting my needs.

Both parents input when raising a child (ren) are vital if the child is to have a balanced view about relationships. Of course, there are exceptions in cases of abuse, death and other uncompromising situations however, wherever possible, children should not be living the experience of the affected parent.

The issue of absent fathers in Black and Minority Ethnic (BME) communities has been an ongoing issue that is still present to date. Many young people do not have a sense of identity due to the absence of a father or a positive male role model in their lives. "A father is someone who further guides the mind of a young child", a father is seen as someone who protects and provides security for his family. The absence of a father in a home may result in a young person looking for security outside the home by older gang leaders and drug dealers for protection. In cases of females, amongst the many whom have become teen mothers, many also lack the understanding about self-value and self-worth and may seek to find safety and protection in other males who are often from broken homes themselves.

A single mother if willing, can be guided to support his/her child through early interventions, such as considering other appropriate males and role models in a child's life. If a single mother does not understand the psychological impact her child is faced with, when growing up without her/ his father's input, this can lead to an emotional disturbance and other consequences.

Scenario 1

A single mother who resents her child's father may consciously or subconsciously cause emotional distress to her child through name-calling and spitefulness due to the child being a direct product of his/her father. A child growing up in this environment may develop challenging behaviour and or low self –esteem as a result of the confusion and anger obtained from his/her experiences at home.

Scenario 2

Some mothers might take delight in the fact that they now have authority and full responsibility for raising their child (ren) in the way they see appropriate. If a mother is in denial of criticism of her child (ren), she becomes defensive when presented with scenarios which might challenge her style of parenting.

For this reason, she may lie for and blame others for her child (ren) mistakes instead of addressing the issue of her parenting style. The issue with this way of parenting is that, the child (ren) can be indoctrinated to believe that women exist for the sole purpose of serving and taking care of men. Such children, (if males) may not have an issue with having children and not taking responsibility for their children even if, they are living in the same household.

In my case, the first scenario is slightly fitting to my experience of growing up with a single mother. However, a bit more complicated. Mum's perception about men stemmed from more than just the hiccups in hers and my dad's relationship. Her views didn't only stem from her view about my father but also my sister's father and another relationship she was in later after her separation with my sister's father. I am not sure if she experienced any other unpleasant relationships before she met my dad but my knowledge of the relationships she had been in, starts with my father. I am not quite sure what relationship my mother had with her father, but I know that her father was separated from her mother and from what I gather it was an acrimonious relationship between her mother and her father. I also know that her grandmother was separated from her grandfather. I do not know the details of any other experiences that may have shaped mums' views about the opposite sex, but I know she was hurt from the way she spoke about men in general.

I can't blame mum for how her experiences shaped my views about the opposite sex as that's what she knew and was her way of protecting me. Mum's views about men whether rightly or wrongly was her truth and her experience which unfortunately wasn't great each time she gave love a go.

Nevertheless, as this book is about my journey, I will not be talking in detail about mum's history or any other person's life because I have not lived it and do not have a full picture. I will only speak based on my experiences and will mention others' stories if there is a link with mine in anyway.

CHAPTER 5

Miss Independent, You Don't Need a Man

Growing up in a single parent home often meant being independent. Mum, my sisters and I would all do things including jobs and activities that society often referenced as a man's job. Let me take you back to what led up to us to moving outside of London and into our new lifestyle with mum as a single parent.

So, I was around fourteen when we moved out of London, the situation that led to the move was the breakdown of marriage between mum and my sister's dad. He was a good man whilst growing up with him, he treated me as one of his own, he was kind and loving from what I remember. I was very fond of him because mum always maintained that he helped her bring me into the UK, so I really appreciated him and was grateful for him from the moment I stepped foot into the UK.

We had a lovely three-bedroom house in London, we lived a good life, we were in a good neighbourhood, had a large garden, which had two sheds and a multi- coloured swing in the back garden. At some point through our stay in London, mum's friend was living with us.

I can't remember if she moved in after I moved to the UK or if she was already living there when I migrated, but I remember that she had sometimes done the cooking and would care for us occasionally. I don't remember much about her relationship with my stepfather, but I do remember a night where there was a big fight. I remember mum screaming and shouting at my stepfather and mums' friend being asked to leave the house. I remember mum picking up an iron underneath the storage below the stairs ready to hit my stepdad with it. I remember sitting down on the stairs holding the house phone ready to call the police. I remember our next-door neighbours standing outside and I remember a close friend of mum's coming over to help make sense of what was happening.

I did not really understand what was happening at the time as I was still young and naive, trying to make sense of this new environment but I knew I was ready to back up mum whatever the case. The allegation at the time was that my stepfather had been having an affair with mum's friend who lived with us.

Following on from this, I remember a new man supporting us with moving from London to Hampshire where we finally settled. I am not quite sure how mum met this new man, but I remember him being very helpful and supportive of mum, myself and my sisters. He supported us with finding a new accommodation, starting a new school and getting settled in our new environment. I am not sure if he was dating my mum prior to us moving out of London or not, but at some point, they were in a relationship, a serious one I would imagine. He was always around helping us with whatever we needed, shopping, taking us to the cinema, you name it he was always available to help.

He was like a father figure to myself and my sisters, I recall him being very easy going and kind, he would often buy things for me and my sisters and would take us out to places to eat. He was educated and appeared to have lived in the UK for a while as he was very familiar with the systems in the UK and didn't have an African twang. He didn't sound like or act like the rest of the African uncles I had come across in my lifetime. He was what I would have considered cool at the time and so did my friends. The reason for this was because he was fun and often advocated on mine and my sister's behalf if we wanted something mum wasn't ready to give us.

As he did not live with us, we regularly experienced the true reality of being children of a single parent. We were reminded of this especially during times where we had to mow the lawn, dismantle beds, paint the walls of our new home and make attempts at fixing broken things in our home. My mum was very proud to say that "I did this" and "without help from any man". This view was subtle to begin with but became more prevalent over time.

Growing up in Hampshire with my sisters and mum as our sole care giver wasn't bad in fact it was good. Mum had a way of making us feel as though we weren't missing out on much without having our fathers around. We had everything we wanted if not instantly then sooner or later we would get it. Compared to the lives of some friends who had grown up with both parents, I can say that we had a better quality of life than they did, in terms of our home environment and presentation in general.

Living in Hampshire was different but good, it lacked diversity and was the kind of place where people would turn to stare when black people walked into a restaurant. You would think that a place like this was very racist but in fact the opposite, most people were very friendly, everyone smiled all the time and they were curious sometimes. Yes, most times we had to travel back into London or Reading to get hair extensions or our traditional foods, but we shopped in bulk, so the trips weren't regular.

CHAPTER 6

A Glimpse into Change

Things began to change concerning mums and my relationship shortly (1-2 years) after we moved to Hampshire. I am not particularly sure what caused a shift in the relationship but for me this started when she asked me to take a pregnancy test at the age of 15, almost in a jokingly forced way with her partner at the time. I didn't find it funny, but did it anyway to prove whatever belief, they had wrong. The reason for this was never explained to me.

At the age of 15, although my interest had begun to peek regarding the opposite sex, it was nothing out of the ordinary. There was a guy I had a crush on at school and I experienced my first kiss on holiday that year. I don't recall any incident that could have caused her to think that I was sexually active, but this is my earliest memory of when I felt mum was starting to act a bit different towards me, but naturally I didn't think deeply into it at the time.

Our relationship begun to deteriorate following on from a house move in Hampshire. I don't remember the exact month or specific date, but I remember being in the lounge (of our second home after the move to Hampshire) with mum listening to a Ghanaian radio station on Sky TV. Mum often listened to these stations to keep up with what was happening in Ghana and in our community, so this was nothing out of the ordinary. The topic presented at the time, was around older relatives (uncles) having sexual relations with their nieces often considerably much younger than they are.

I remember mum and I discussing how awful we felt about such matters, and how appalled we felt about the fact that such issues were silenced in our communities despite the significant harm it causes to young girls. We talked about how the relatives got away with it because the parents of the affected children didn't speak up, but rather sided with the perpetrators and silenced the victim often the child in order to protect the family name and for the sake of not "airing dirty laundry"

My Reflective Account about Silenced Issues Affecting Black and Minority Ethnic Communities

"What happens in the family stays in the family" is one of a few statements often reinforced within Black Minority and Ethnic (BME) groups. The notion of staying silent about issues portrayed as "cultural" or issues causing significant harm to children and their families is very common. Phrases such as the above and others such as "don't air your dirty laundry" is commonly promoted in such communities but at what cost?

Sexual exploitation and abuse, domestic violence, forced marriage, mental illness, female genital mutilation and emotional unavailability are just a few examples of issues often silenced within many BME communities. From what I have noticed about how such issues are dealt with in many BME communities, I am not surprised at the fact that people stay silent about such issues.

The stigma associated with issues such as mental health, rape and sexual abuse alone is enough to cause victims to stay silent as it is easier that way. At times, victims are labelled as promiscuous in cases of sexual assault and in cases of mental health, victims are talked about in a demeaning way with the use of terms such as "mad" and "crazy".

When it comes to mental health, religion drives a lot of the stigma that victims' face. Often it is assumed that a victim is possessed by an evil spirit that needs to be cast out. Though I understand this way of thinking, I feel that it is somewhat ignorant as it does not take into account many other earthly factors such as drugs (which can induce mental illnesses) and life events (divorce, death, debt, crisis) which, can contribute to an unstable mental wellbeing.

Low self -esteem, social exclusion and isolation are just a few of the lasting impact of stigmas victims might encounter which of course, could escalate if not monitored. Aside from the stigmas faced in own communities, victims face additional barriers such as untailored services to meet their cultural needs, ethical needs and institutionalised racism which, in itself can cause further emotional and psychological hiccups.

I feel that challenging and re-evaluating some of the generational beliefs and values indoctrinated within our communities is a way to start addressing these issues. Do not be afraid to challenge people when you hear them call others "crazy" or "mad" if suffering from a mental illness or displaying behaviours not considered as the "norm". Do not be afraid to explore and probe further into people's behaviours. Instead of branding a young person as promiscuous, why don't you seek to understand the reasons behind the behaviours, could it be that they were (and still are) abused at a young age? Could it be, that they are trying to seek the attention they are not getting at home? Could it be that they are trying to communicate something, but don't know how to?

We need to start asking questions and start talking about these issues instead of silencing them, this is how awareness will be raised. When awareness is raised, it increases the chances of creating and receiving tailored support to meet our needs. Listening to individuals affected instead of dismissing, judging, labelling and shaming them as well as professional and self-education through online learning and resources about the impact of such practices is also an effective way of addressing this problem.

Harmful cultural and silenced practices within BME communities have sadly caused a lot of emotional, physical and psychological damage to many children and young people, which has translated into troubled adulthood. Albert Bandura's bobo doll experiment evidenced that children learn through observation and imitation, so unless we give children and young people examples of positive behaviours to observe and imitate, silenced practices such as the above mentioned will remain silenced.

CHAPTER 7

The Change

I don't remember the exact timeline but at some point, weeks, maybe months after listening to the discussion on the radio with mum, she began to accuse me of having sexual relations with her partner at the time. It didn't make sense. From talking about how we felt about such matters, to being accused about partaking in it, I was just as confused as her partner was, hence why he approached my aunties living in London for support.

I wasn't sure why mum thought this or what triggered this accusation as my relationship with her partner was the same as my sister's relationship with him. He was like a father figure to us, yet I was singled out. Was it something I had said or done, was it something he had said or done, was it anxiety from the radio discussion, what was it?

To date, I still don't know what triggered this accusation and may never know but I do know that things were changing very fast, too fast for me to manage or even process. The days, months and years following this felt very heavy and were life changing.

The accusations of having sexual relations with her partner didn't stop there, there was accusation of theft, lying, jealousy and envy. Life at home, was no longer the same, my relationship with mum and my sisters were no longer the same. The place I called home was suddenly tense and uncomfortable. At times, mum and I would go for days without talking because everything said would somehow turn hostile.

It hurt me that my sisters who were very young at the time were exposed to such chaos. It hurt me that their perception of me could change due to the situation at hand. The days of me helping mum with deciding on outfits to wear to events, now turned into her comments about me being envious and jealous of her. I began to distance myself. I was there when she needed me but wouldn't voluntarily be there for the sake of protecting my emotions and my heart.

Slowly, I began to build a lot of resentment in my heart towards mum. Every time we clashed my heart felt so heavy and bitter, to the point where I would question if she was my mum because I struggled to understand how she could carry on with such damaging accusations towards her own child, despite being aware of how I was being impacted.

At some point during this season in my life, I made a deal with myself to never allow my children to go through this and still stand by this self-proclamation, simply because I knew what it felt like to feel rejected and neglected.

Things got from bad to worse. I began staying out later after college to avoid being home, I went out with friends drinking and my grades at college began to drop dramatically. I knew I needed the grades to get into university because that was the only way I could escape my troubles at home, if not permanently then at least for a long period of time. Although, I was very much aware of this and had figured out that going to university was an achievable plan to help me leave home, I still struggled as I was heavily distracted mentally and emotionally by what was happening at home.

I remember one weekday morning, whereby I had told mum that I will be staying out a bit later with some friends after college. Around 6pm, I had a call from mum asking me where I was , I responded by saying "remember I said to you that I will be staying out after college, didn't I?", she then told me to come home which I thought was a bit unfair considering she had already agreed to it that morning. But I said goodbye to my friends and made my way home. I could sense that she wasn't in a good mood, but I was somewhat use to this, so I didn't make much of it.

When I got home, she was in the kitchen cooking, I went into the kitchen and said hello to her as usual, her response to the hello was to shout at me. Initially, I did not understand why she was shouting and what I had done wrong.

She then proceeded to say that I was rude to her over the phone by saying "didn't I?". Mum proceeded to hit me around the face and all over my body followed by the pulling of my hair extensions so tightly that I could feel the pain on my scalp. As I was crying and shouting whilst asking her to stop, I couldn't help but notice my younger sisters in the living room next door. Although, they shut the door so that they couldn't witness what was happening, they heard it all and I know it wasn't pleasant for them. Eventually, I managed to get away from her grip and run upstairs to my room for safety and shut my door in hopes that she wouldn't come in.

The thought that my sisters may have perceived me in a different way, is something I battled with regularly. I was their big sister and they were my little sisters, not knowing how they saw me due to what mum had told them about me, was unsettling.

When I first came to the UK, my youngest sister was the age of 1 and the middle sister, 6. There was a 5-year gap between the three of us, but our relationship was never catty when growing up, we complimented each other well and got on nicely.

The second born, I will describe as one with a gentle nature, she didn't say much but was very observant. When she did decide to speak however, you always laughed and wanted her to carry on speaking for as long as possible. She knew how to banter, and she complimented her humour with elements of sarcasm. She was very tall, slim built and had a beautiful smile. Some thought she was shy, but I don't think this was ever the case. She just liked her own company (maybe a bit too much) and said no to things which she didn't feel like participating in.

The youngest one also very tall with slender legs was a character, even from a very young age, she was the life and soul of the party, very vibrant with a care-free spirit. One to cheer you up easily on a sad day with a silly comment or action that left you with no choice but to cheer up. She was the type to give you a sales pitch that made you buy things you didn't even know you wanted. We all had different personalities but combined resulted in a lot of banter and laughter.

I remember memories from some evenings where we would blast out music in our living room with the lights off and all doors closed dancing to migraine shank and heads shoulders knees and toes. Although I was a laid-back sister with strict tendency's (when mum was on holiday and I was given charge over the house), I'd like to think that they looked up to me based on some of my greater characteristics such as my determination to succeed and my playful nature.

The conversations, accusations, tears and arguments they witnessed throughout the years deeply saddened me. Did they see me as a role model? Were they hesitant about sharing parts of their lives with me due to the need to side with mum? Were they directly affected by it too? We never spoke about this or how they felt about everything they witnessed at home.

I remember crying out to God in a lot of pain several times with no response. I never questioned his existence due to my childhood experiences of him, but I questioned if he cared about me because I didn't hear from him when I needed him the most. Maybe that's why my relationship with God deteriorated over time, I asked him to somehow let mum believe me or somehow let the truth come out, but days went by, then months and years and still no response.

Through these questioning and bargaining sessions with God, I began to question if all this would be happening if my father was around. This season in my life drew me to get angrier at my father and reinforced mum's portrayal of the type of man he was, one who didn't care about his child. I felt that maybe if he called more or made more of an effort to know me, he would maybe sense that something wasn't right at home, but this didn't happen, and I didn't say anything either. I mean, how could I? how would I even have started the conversation with the man I hadn't seen in years and only texted or called each other during birthdays and Christmas celebrations?

Although, mum never mentioned this incident or showed any remorse about what she had done, she knew that she had gone too far this time as I overheard a conversation, she was having with someone on the phone. She was talking about how bad she felt for hitting me like that and was discussing whether to say something about it but the other person on the phone discouraged this as she was the mother and I was the child (another common response often reinforced in BME homes). So, she didn't bring this up and we just carried on as though nothing happened. However, this incident was significant to me because my mum wasn't the type of parent to hit us. This was my first and last experience of being hit by mum.

As time went by, the cloud over my head and the burden of everything got heavier. There was no one I could talk to about what was happening and nowhere to turn due to the notion of "what happens in the family stays in the family". I was isolated and had no family nearby; I couldn't go to my aunts for support either as for years the relationship between them and my mum had always been unstable. Mums relationship with her sisters was unpredictable, at times the relationship was great and at other times they would go for months without saying anything to each other. Mum often talked about being the black sheep when growing up, so I didn't dare think to ask them for help. The idea of speaking to them about what was happening at home felt like a betrayal towards mum, so I didn't.

However, there was a family friend who tried to help but her support was cut short by mum when she began to advocate for me. She was the only one who truly understood me, I was able to cry to her and express that I didn't understand what was going on. I even remember her telling mum to be careful as this chaotic environment could cause me to seek out for assurance and safety elsewhere (in a man) but as previously stated, mum cut contact and warned me not to contact her again. So, I never spoke to her or saw her again.

The chaos and commotion at home eventually took a toll on mum too as she was admitted to hospital with a minor stroke. I don't remember the full details on the day of the stroke, but I remember when I went to see her at the hospital with my sisters, she was laying down on the bed unable to move one side of her body. She was paralysed on her left side from face to toe which also affected her speech.

Even though, still hurt by what had been going on between myself and mum, I felt sorry for mum and struggled to fathom how a strong, independent woman became helpless overnight. The sight of mum helpless caused a feeling of unease in the hospital room due to the silence of not knowing what to say or think. Although helpless, I could see the determination in her eyes to communicate with us. Mum eventually slurred out her desire for us to read her a bible scripture. The verse read:

Psalm 54 New International Version (NIV)

1 Save me, O God, by your name; vindicate me by your might.

2 Hear my prayer, O God; listen to the words of my mouth.

3 Strangers are attacking me; ruthless men seek my life-- men without regard for God. Selah

4 Surely God is my help; the Lord is the one who sustains me.

5 Let evil recoil on those who slander me; in your faithfulness destroy them.

6 I will sacrifice a freewill offering to you; I will praise your name, O LORD, for it is good.

7 For he has delivered me from all my troubles, and my eyes have looked in triumph on my foes.

Seeing mum helpless brought tears to my eyes, as I could no longer recognise the active, independent parent I grew up with. I did what I knew which was to pray for her with my sisters using the verse we read whilst holding onto any faith we had left in hopes that things would be okay. Time went by and mum was eventually discharged home, requiring support to walk and with daily task. She was discharged with the knowledge that a physiotherapist and an occupational therapist will be assessing her to determine appropriate support to meet her needs at home.

By this time, we had already begun to discuss the plan for me to take my sisters to school as mum could no longer drive. We also begun to discuss the possibility of putting my college education on hold, to support mum at home, if needed. The thought of this upset me as it meant that I would also have to postpone going to university.

Although during this period things had settled down at home due to mum's wellbeing, I knew it was temporary. I did not show how upset I was because I knew my sisters and mum needed me and we had no-one else around to take on that type of responsibility.

Miraculously, after about two sessions of taking my sisters to school, then making my way to college, I witnessed my first ever miracle. I often heard about miracles and watched them on TV, but I had never witnessed and certainly not had one in my own home. A group of elders from church came over to visit and pray for mum which was a normal practice conduct in most of the churches we had come across, if a member was not well. I remember guiding them to her room where we stood around her to pray for her, as we were praying, I felt cold air in the room but thought nothing of it. After about ten maybe fifteen minutes of prayer, mum began to talk, her speech was back, and she was no longer paralysed on one side of her body.

I recall her running back home after she walked the elders back to their cars. It was the first time I had seen a miracle in person, I didn't know what to make of it, but I was happy that mum was back to her normal self and about life not feeling so foreign anymore. Although I witnessed a miracle in my own home, a part of me wasn't satisfied with the idea that God cared about me as my prayers were unanswered. It felt like my relationship with mum would become hostile again. I was still hurting, I felt alone, I was alone, and had learnt to be there for myself emotionally and mentally. It was as though I had stopped myself from feeling things, I stopped showing emotions and my tears became less and rare. It was as though my emotions had channelled into resentment and internal anger which often bubbled up in the form of a minor heart burn when I thought about the accusations made against me.

I was at the point where, I no longer recognised mum when I looked into her eyes. I did not see the mum I met for the first time when I was 11. The mum I use to go everywhere with, whom I was close to and looked up to. I felt judgement when I looked into her eyes, I didn't recognise her because I could no longer predict her. One day things would be fine, and we would laugh but always with caution as another day, she would accuse me of certain things, and I would be the target of her frustration.

Mum and I never sat down to address this until many years after, sometimes we just got on with life as though nothing had happened although things were not the same and other times, accusations of theft and jealously would cause me to regress emotionally.

CHAPTER 8

The Guy in The Grey Tracksuit

"This chaotic environment could cause me to seek out for assurance and safety in a man". These were the words uttered by mum's friend before we lost contact. I met a guy during the unsettling season. I met him on my way home after my afternoon class at college.

When I saw him, I didn't really think much of him except that he was black, tall with dark skin, built in stature and did not look local. He was wearing a grey tracksuit and walked with a slight bop, ahead of me. When I walked through the tunnel and up the stairs, he was already there waiting for me. He approached me and introduced himself. From how he spoke, it was evident that he was from London. We talked for a bit and he mentioned that he had recently moved into the area and confirmed that he was from London. We exchanged numbers and agreed to see each other again.

As time went by, I saw him most days after college, we would talk about his life and mine but I never dared to mention what was happening at home. I also began to question him about why he had to be home by seven o'clock when he talked about taking me out on a date. This is when he informed me that he was in the area awaiting a prison trial for dealing heroin and was on tag hence why his curfew was at seven o'clock.

Something about this guy intrigued me. Although, I knew he was no good for me, I was beginning to like him. It could have been because he was older than me and seemed mature in comparison to the guys I had liked before or, it could have been due to his lifestyle being able to distract me from my own. I don't know what it was about him, but I began to really enjoy being in his company. When I was with him, I wasn't thinking about home or anything else.

He was very honest about his life and mentioned that he had connections at a university, he visited regularly. This thrilled me as this university, he spoke of, was at the top of the list of universities I wanted to attend, in due time. I remember the conversation following on from the night, I gave myself to him. I looked up at him and said to him "I bet you are one of those guys who don't call girls back". He laughed and said no and that he wanted to carry on seeing me and wanted us to meet again the following day.

Turns out I was right because I never heard from him the following day and didn't see him around anymore. I made no attempts to go by his place either because I thought that he made his intentions very clear and known.

CHAPTER 9

The Light Bulb Moment

Meanwhile, at college a visit from two police officers who came to question me about the accusations made by mum caused one of my lecturers to sense that something was wrong. He offered his support and said to me kindly, to talk to him if needed. I told him that I was fine but acknowledged his offer. The accusations at home escalated so much, to the point that it wasn't only about mums' partner but also her male friends, whom she banned from coming to our house. Mum accused me of going to parties, I hadn't even been aware off, stating that 'a friend' had called her to tell her that he/she saw me there dancing inappropriately.

She accused me of talking behind her back to her friends, telling people that I hated her and that she was a bad mother. As a result, she banned me from talking to any of her friends and accused me of telling the police officers, who interviewed me, that I said she "does not wish me well". A statement regularly brought up every time we had a disagreement.

At this point, I was so numb to everything due to all the emotional blows I had endured, that I came across as unbothered (which probably translated as me being rude in mums' eyes).

At some point throughout this season of my life, my college grades had begun to cause me some anxieties. I wondered whether I would still make it to university the following year. I was partying, drinking and beginning to associate myself with some negative influences. I got into a fight with some girls during a house party and conflicted with another girl at college over her boyfriend. I wasn't in the right headspace and this was translated in my behaviours outside of home. At home, I kept to myself and did what was required, for me to have a stress-free life.

I remember a day when mum approached me and said that she had been to the council and had booked an appointment for me to be rehoused elsewhere. She told me to attend, if I wanted to leave home. It was out of the blue, and I seriously considered it as it seemed like a way out, but I didn't attend the appointment and decided to remain home.

Reflecting on this, I may have chosen to remain home because I was aware of the reality of the council's system, through some of the people I was associated with at the time. One person I use to hang around with, was in the system and I knew it was likely that I would be placed in a hostel, (often also housed with alcohol and drug users) before getting my own accommodation. For this reason, I concluded that remaining at home was the better option. Despite everything happening, it was a safer environment.

I still remember the lightbulb moment which forced me back on track academically. I had skipped a college class to go to the park with a friend one weekday afternoon. It was nearing the end of term, so we started to discuss what our plans were after we left college. She mentioned that she was not yet sure about what she would be doing but, probably get a job and mentioned that she had inheritance, a loved one had left for her when they passed away.

During our conversation, I observed that she was not focused and did not come across as though she had a plan. It came across as though she had money set aside for her, and she had options about what she wanted to do after college. This is when it hit me, I didn't have savings, I didn't have a wealthy dying family member and certainly didn't have a job that could fund me that long. In fact, the only choice I had at the time, which would accommodate my needs was to go to university. That talk with her, is what I needed to put me back on track.

Following on from this, I began to put more effort into my assignments and sought for help continuously from lecturers when needed. The final year of college was very challenging, but I was determined to get my life sorted out. Despite all the determination I had, I couldn't escape the stares and snares I got from people in the library who had heard about the fight I had gotten into and from the friends of the girl I conflicted with over her boyfriend.

There were times I'd walk past a group of girls who would laugh or say something out loud, but I never showed how scared I was or how much I was affected. I would walk past them with my head held high and kept focused on my goal to get my grade high again. I knew that if I didn't get into university, I would be home for a much longer period which seemed much more uncomfortable to me in comparison to the snare and stares I got at college. Staying home for an additional year after 3 years of college was not an option I was willing to entertain. So, I worked hard and pushed myself until I was certain university was an option again.

After many prayers by myself, with mum and the phone calls made to pastors back home, as well as money mum sent to them to pray for me to get into university. I was so excited to find out that I had been accepted into my first choice of university to study social work.

Social work is a course I initially did not even consider due to how the media had portrayed it. I wanted to be a dental hygienist as I liked the idea of owning my own practice, however, after a failed interview at a different university I knew it was a difficult course to get into, especially with a BTEC diploma.

Now that I think about it, part of me feels that mum may have been encouraging of me doing social work due to her experience with a social worker, whom I only met once after I got home from college one day. I don't know what she was supporting mum with at the time but my excitement about leaving home caused me to start buying and packing my things, six months in advance.

My part time job as a sales assistant funded most of the things I bought and needed. I wouldn't say that I was excited about the course I had been accepted to study but rather the idea of having an independent life away from home. A chance to start life again without judgement and/or people's knowledge about my history.

CHAPTER 10

A New Life, A New Me

I still remember the day he called me, I think I was getting ready to go somewhere when my phone rang. I looked at the number and I didn't recognise it as a local number. I picked up, and on the other side of it was Jordan the guy I had met by the tunnel, over a year ago. I was very shocked to hear his voice and to hear from him, he immediately explained that he was not able to call me or see me the following day as discussed, over a year ago, as he was sentenced the night, we planned on seeing each other.

We talked about how he had been and what it was like in prison. He told me that he had gotten into a fight and talked about some of the struggles he was facing there. He also mentioned some positive memories and the hustles he had learnt so far. To begin with, our conversations were just about giving each other updates about our lives but this eventually turned into conversations and plans about being in a relationship upon his return.

We talked about plans to visit some holiday destinations, he had seen on TV or in a booklet whilst in prison and talked about the things we would like to do together.

The more we talked, the more we grew to like each other again. I told him that I had been accepted into the university he visited regularly, and he told me that he would be out in a year's time. He shared some intimate parts of his life with me, his genuine and persistent approach caused me to believe that we could work and very well indeed.

Although a year was a long time to wait for him, I was willing and planning on doing so. The more I spoke to him, our plans felt real. I developed strong and deep emotions for him although we didn't see each other physically. He made a request for me to visit him and I thought about it several times, but I was not brave enough to go through with it. For this reason, our communication was purely dependent on telephone calls and letter contact which I requested for him to post to a friend's address to avoid further conflict at home.

The non-physical relationship we had allowed us to connect deeper emotionally. I talked about him to my friends and would wait patiently by the phone to receive his calls. To me, he was very honest, genuine, tough and caring. To me, he was a representation of someone who could protect me, for this reason, I was more than willing to put aside his history. I convinced myself into thinking that everyone makes mistakes and dealing drugs does not take away from the fact that he was a good man.

Things at home with mum had gotten somewhat better, we were not in conflict as much but there were still a lot of things unsaid and lot of things unaddressed. Some days were good and other days not so good. I would say that at this point, I was use to the changing atmosphere at home but not to this new perception of mum that I had witnessed, all these years. I was still unable to predict her and was still very much confused about how we got to where we were.

The day of moving to university finally came and I was overjoyed. I was dropped off by mum, my sisters and a friend who assisted me with putting things in order when we arrived. Afterwards, we went to the seaside to spend a bit of time together before they left. I remember sitting in my room thinking to myself, now what? I was looking forward to my new environment and was excited about the prospect that no one knew me, my story or my history. It was a fresh start for me and a chance to put my mind to rest after years of feeling unsettled.

Life was going well, the distractions of being in a new place, alongside meeting new people and getting familiar with my surroundings buried and suppressed the hurt I had gone through for years. My phone call exchange with Jordan carried on for a short while before he told me the crushing news. His time had been extended as he was caught with a phone and was not due to be out for another year. Part of me was very frustrated with this because of our plans. Being together didn't look possible however, I knew that he was risking an extension on his sentence, every time we spoke, which is why part of me felt that I owed it to him to wait.

Eventually, I decided to move on. Surprisingly, he was very understanding when I told him this and that I had met someone else. We agreed to stay friends and limited our contact but still communicated with each other occasionally due to the bond we had built.

CHAPTER 11

Same Guys Different Suits

The new guy I had met at university was someone I had met a couple of months back through a school friend at a bus station. I was surprised to see him at the same university I attended, and we began to develop a friendship. This eventually transpired into something more, so we decided to give, being in a relationship, a go. He treated me well, we laughed a lot together and enjoyed being in each other's company. Some days we argued and other days we were inseparable, this was my first adult relationship and I was beginning to learn a lot about myself.

I think part of me loved him, but I wasn't fully invested in our relationship and he knew that. This was simply me putting in practice, what I had heard mum say over the years about not trusting men and "putting one foot in and one foot out" so that I don't get hurt. I was about 70% invested and 30% protected.

I had put a deadline on our relationship without his knowledge from the moment we became official, I was willing to give things a go for a year only, then end it regardless of his or my feelings at the time. I cannot explain why this was my thinking, but I guess it gives you a preview of how I valued relationships with the opposite sex. I had mastered how to have full control of my emotions by that time and saw men as accessories, metaphorically. With or without them, my outfit looked good, they were of use but not a necessity.

There was something about this new guy that didn't really sit too well with me throughout our relationship, but it didn't bother me enough to investigate. He always had two phones and somehow managed to magically get money instantly, when needed. He denied being a drug dealer although admitted to being involved with it previously. I didn't get much out of him when I made attempts to explore where the money came from but as mentioned, it didn't bother me enough to probe further.

In line with my pessimism, our relationship was cut short after 10 months. The cause of what ended the relationship was a bit of a blur. We didn't deliberately separate but the circumstance at the time caused the separation. It was the last day of my first year at university.

Whilst packing, I heard a knock on my door, when answered I saw three men standing there who introduced themselves as the police. They advised that they were looking for him and confirmed that I was his girlfriend. The officers showed me a CCTV image of him and began to question me me about where he was and our relationship before asking to search my room. I questioned what he had done and why they were looking for him, with no informative response. Although I explained to them that I had not seen him due to an argument that took place the night before, the truth was that he was hiding in a friend's clothing cupboard two doors away from me. We had, gotten into an argument the night before, but I had seen him earlier on that morning in his friends' room and was still upset with him. The truth was that when they asked me to call him (with the officer's present), I deliberately rang an old phone number, I knew wasn't in use anymore.

With no luck, the officers gave me their contact details and asked me to call them when I heard from him. When I shut my door, I broke down in tears, many questions ran through my head about what he could have been involved in, with no idea, yet many possibilities of what it may have been. When we eventually saw each other in the corridor shortly after the encounter, he thanked me but didn't tell me what had happen despite my attempts to find out. This was the last time I saw him.

Events following this was me trying to seek answers from him concerning why he was wanted over the summer holidays through text and calls with no luck. We attempted to meet up, but our schedules didn't cooperate. At some point I stopped hearing from him, no response to calls, texts, post or email. When I returned to university for my second year, he wasn't there. I didn't know where he was, I still hadn't heard from him and when friends asked me about where he was, I was unable to answer their question.

I decided to focus more on socialising and self-discovery through the rest of my time at university. Although I went on dates, I was already clear in my mind that I didn't want things to progress. It was as though, I just liked the idea of meeting people but nothing more.

One thing I noticed through this season of my life, was the type of guys who were attracted to me. Almost all if not all of them were involved with some form of criminal activity, mostly drugs. I didn't know why I kept attracting these kinds of men. When I made deliberate attempts to date different types of guys, sooner or later, I found out that they were involved with some form of criminality. This was pretty much my experience with dating throughout the rest of my university life.

CHAPTER 12

Resurfaced Emotions

University was still very much enjoyable for me, I made new friends and kept in touch with the old ones I had met from my first year. Myself and one of my housemates alongside some other friends from first year, managed to find another day better suited for us to go out clubbing as the normal weekdays were no longer working due to placement. This allowed us to mingle with the locals and gave us the opportunity to explore other areas of the city.

We met new people and just adapted our lives to suit our schedules. At times, we had girl's night in where we just drank, and talked about the guys we had been on dates with and gave updates about our lives. Other nights we attended house parties or went out for dinners. We were living our best lives, with somewhat minimal drama and a lot of fun and memories.

Home life had also improved a bit, in my opinion due to the distance between myself and mum. I went home around late December a couple of days before Christmas and always came back early to avoid any issues and did the same with other holidays. I went home when I was needed to help with somethings, but I wasn't the type to go home every week like other fellow students.

Despite that, things were better at home and my university life was great, sometimes emotions from my hurt surfaced back up. I did not mention to anyone what I had gone through at home all these years due to fear of judgement and not being believed. It was at the point that it dawned on me how imperative it was for me to be believed. I often contemplated seeking counselling support but the small voice at the back of my mind always stopped me in doing so by constantly reminding me about how "what happens in the family stays in the family". For this reason, I never did seek counselling and just dealt with my emotions as and when they came mostly, by ignoring them.

Thoughts of what I had gone through still caused me to feel so bitter towards mum. The more I thought about things the angrier I felt so by the end of my second year, I had already made up my mind up that I wasn't going to move back home after my degree. The plan was to secure a job during my placement year and remain in the city where I was attending university. I was happy with that plan and worked towards it.

CHAPTER 13

Everything is Permissible, but Not Everything is Beneficial

At some point during my second year Jordan was released from prison and came to see me. We caught up on conversation and missed experiences and his plans moving forward. Months following this, consisted of us going back and forth about us and where we stand. It was very clear and evident that he was ready to be in a relationship with me. He had maintained this throughout our conversation a year after I met him, and I knew he was serious.

Although some of my feelings for him came rushing back when I saw him again, I couldn't commit to us being in a relationship as we had previously discussed. Was it because I had already decided in my mind that I did not want a relationship earlier on that year? Or was it something else?

I didn't see him all the time, but when I did see him, he often stayed around for a couple of days to make some money. I was saddened by the fact that he went back to selling drugs despite, his enthusiasm shown during our conversations about his commitment to live a different lifestyle. Part of me felt frustrated with his decision to return to selling drugs but another part of me understood that the criminal justice system was not created in favour of young black men and with no job prospects for him based on his record, his options were limited.

I expressed my concerns and dislike for what he did but then again, I understood, and he knew that any slip ups meant he'd be back in prison, possibly for longer as he was on probation. As I hadn't given him a direct answer about where we were with our relationship it remained a "situationship" for months. I would see him, we would order some food or go out and get some food, we would chill in my room or in his space at the time and watch something.

At some point he introduced me to friends and even family which again reinforced how serious he was about us. He always claimed that I was the type of girl he needed and began to parade around the idea of marriage, but only briefly. I maintained the idea that he was a good guy but was unable to give him a valid reason about why I didn't want to progress our relationship further.

I felt like a hypocrite as I didn't want to be in a relationship with him, but I didn't want to let go of him either. I thought about us very hard and long, repeatedly, I eventually identified my reasons for not wanting to progress things. I knew he was serious about us so getting in a relationship with him would have potentially led to something long term, and for this reason I was very careful to consider all possible outcomes of a relationship with him. My reason for not pursuing us was because he wasn't determined enough to work hard for a different lifestyle.

He made promises and talked of plans to get a legal job, become a personal trainer and even pursue his music interest but weeks, months and years went by with no evidence of this. Another reason was the fact that I was unable to predict his movement. Contact with him was uncertain at times. I would see him some months and he would disappear other months then reappear out of nowhere. When questioned about this the answer was always to do with some trouble, he had gotten himself into. If it wasn't being stabbed by a group of young people who were looking at him wrongly, it was about causing an accident when driving without a license. It felt as though my future and my children's (if we got to that point) future would be uncertain and unsettling with him. I didn't want an absent father in my children's life.

I felt conflicted whilst thinking about the possible outcomes of a relationship with him because, when I was with him, I saw past the above reasons because he was a good guy, one who cared deeply for me and one who treated me so well. Jordan had a way with me, all worries and anxieties about my home life, all my hesitations were put on hold and almost forgotten about. This was until something happened which brought back to memory how emotionally drained, I felt at times. Not knowing if he was okay; if he was alive or dead; if he was back in prison; how our future will work out; if my family would ever accept him; and how we would raise our children when their father's presence would be uncertain made me feel uneasy.

All these questions caused me so much stress and often quickly knocked me back into reality. The fact was, I knew we could be good together, but we were not made for each other. Our dreams and aspirations would not yoke together, we were just not compatible for each other.

CHAPTER 14

A Lost Soul and The Encounter

Much like most students, I was drained by my final year of university and couldn't wait to finish. Things were not as enjoyable as they were in the first and second year due to being on placement for a much longer time. By this time, I was attending university once a week and worked four days a week at placement. It felt as though I was working fulltime and then cramming in fulltime studies, on the one day. This was never enough time to do my assignments, so most of my weekends were spent in the university library catching up on academic reading and revisiting lecturer's online notes.

I was looking forward to finishing university as I was ready to get into the next stage of my life. I'd often heard that life begins after university as you get to work and earn money, so was looking forward to this new life I was getting ready to embark on.

I began to plan my next move and started to enquire about possible job prospects at my placement. Unfortunately, there were no adverts at the time, so I began to apply for other jobs locally, then jobs a bit out of the area, still with the intention of not moving back home. I finally got offered a job role which excited me as my plans were coming together. I had passed my driving test in January, a couple of months earlier and was due to graduate. Things were looking up and I was in a happy place in my life with the exception that internally, I felt empty and broken. I didn't know what it was, I didn't feel content or satisfied with my new upcoming life but was unable to explain why.

As I sat at the edge of my bed, I began to reflect on all the things going well in my life. I thought about my career, marriage, owing a home and having children which all seemed great, however, I kept saying to myself "there has to be more to life". The only issue was, I didn't know what this "more" looked like or where I could find it.

I had always known that I wanted to get married, in fact, I desired to get married but didn't believe that marriages could last forever, as intended by God. I hadn't really seen any positive examples of marriages around me or heard about the benefits of it. When marriage was talked about in my community, it was often along the lines of the tolerance required due to two different people, their cultures, morals and principles coming together, which I would imagine wasn't an easy task. Someone around me described marriage as a contract between two people as though it was a job. This view of marriage combined with my perception about men growing up in the environment that I did, as well as my limited contact with my dad all reinforced my disbelief about marriage being a lasting covenant. I was very angry and frustrated with dad around this time in my life, I felt as though he made no efforts to even know me and yet again, will be missing another significant stage in my life, graduation.

This frustration often took my mind back to an experience with him, when I around 16 years old. At this age, I made a phone call to dad and asked him to buy me a laptop to support my studies, after mum said she couldn't help due to limited funds. Dad's response was that he didn't have the money and that I had to remember that he had my brothers to look after also. Although disappointed, the part of his statement which stuck with me was, the fact that he reminded me about having my brothers to look after.

How the statement was framed, made me feel as though my brothers needs took priority over mine when, we all should have been of the same priority (even though I didn't live with him). I was hurt by the statement and felt that he could have managed the situation better with his response, as his response to me that day only emphasised mums' portrayal about him not taking responsibility of me as his child all these years.

The experiences concerning my relationships and the views I had acquired over time led me to think that, "I want to get married but will be okay if it doesn't work and ends in divorced as I have seen mum do it and cope well, so I can manage too".

So, although I had this desire to get married one day, you could somewhat say my mentality about marriage at the time was setting me up for failure. It was as though I had already planned on it failing and I was content with that. What I wasn't content with, was the fact that my life at the time including my dreams and aspirations for the future didn't seem complete. I wasn't content with just working, owning a home, a car, and having children. My spirit was yearning for more and completeness.

This unsettling feeling and compelling disturbance of an incomplete life is what caused me to go to church. I don't know why I thought to go to church as I didn't think it would give me answers, but I did anyway. Throughout my three years at university, I hardly went to church, in fact, looking back at it I can count how many times I went on one hand. I went a few times during my first year at university, but I didn't have any encounters or experiences to keep me in any of the churches I had attended. As mentioned at the beginning of this book, I grew up with church all around me and even had personal encounters with God at a young age, but the lack of response from God when I cried to him for help, pushed me so far away from him to a point where I didn't even know where my bible was and had somewhat forgotten how to pray. I claimed I was a Christian and my friends knew that but now looking back at it, this was probably done to reassure myself that God existed and to sugar-coat my lifestyle at the time.

The God portrayed to me when I was a child growing up in Ghana was an almighty God, he wasn't someone you could just talk to about anything, you spoke to him about the big stuff and tried your best to live a sin free life. When I got older, I concluded that I wasn't perfect due to the sins I had committed and was still committing but God knew my heart and knew that I was trying.

I had sex before marriage, I lied, watched porn, insulted people, I clubbed, smoked sometimes, but I was a good person and didn't commit the big sins. I wasn't a killer, I didn't commit adultery or do some of the big things the 10 commandments talked about. I figured that as I helped the homeless and people who needed my help despite my sins, I would still go to heaven because I wasn't too bad, compared to others.

One early Sunday morning after clubbing out late the night before, I decided to go to a church. I looked at churches and came across one online which a friend had told me about, a while back. I decided to give it a go and made it to the morning service a bit late. I was ushered to a seat at the front (I didn't want to sit at the front, but I guess that's what happens when you turn up late, you don't get much choice about the seating plan) just before they began worship.

Reluctantly standing at the front row, I mumbled throughout the worship songs not recognising any of them. Fortunately, this was for a short period of time, so I was certain no one noticed my mumbles. I was instantly engaged with the sermon due to the content shared.

The preacher was a white British male who was married to a black African female. The preacher talked about the challenges and struggles they faced as an interracial couple in relation to their belief in Christ and how they overcame the challenges faced. Following on from the sermon, there was what I now know as an alter call (a call to give one's life to Christ, this consisted of a prayer confessing with your mouth that Jesus is lord, and believing in your heart that he had died for your sins). Whilst the piano was playing, there was a talk about the feeling of loss and emptiness (which I could identified with) and how this void can be filled by Jesus the messiah. I don't know what happened to me but as I stood and listened to the message it felt as though Jesus had the answers to the questions, which had been going on through my mind, for a while. It felt as though he could help me fill the void I had in my heart or at least lead me to a place where it could be filled.

I suddenly got overwhelmed with everything and began to cry uncontrollably uttering "I am here" repeatedly. I did not know what was going on, I felt so embarrassed at the thought that people next to me could hear me cry. Shortly after the encounter I was ushered to a back room where my contact details were taken down. Throughout the following weeks I received calls, from staff at the church, but I never responded. I was so confused and embarrassed about the experience that took place, so I decided never to step foot in that church again, and I didn't. This encounter never left me though, I kept thinking about it repeatedly and somewhat prayed and spoke to God about it.

Intrigued by what had happen, I was now in a state of trying to find a way to balance my old lifestyle with this new experience, with no avail. For this reason, I decided to seek for further guidance through the bible, the only issue was that I didn't have one. This is what led me to make a deal with God. As a student trying to survive on a loan, I was not ready to pay for a bible, so I asked God to provide me one for free in exchange for my belief in the encounter being of him.

Following on from this, I googled local churches near my house, the plan was to walk in and ask for a bible. I visited two churches one Sunday morning, one was bolted, and the other was not yet opened so I went back home with no intentions of returning. However, I kept reminding God about my free bible to reassure me the experience was from him, as though it was for his benefit. I am not sure about the timeline between when I reminded God about the free bible and when I actually got the free bible, but I was walking in town with a housemate and came across a Jehovah witness stand.

A woman was giving out their booklet as usual, we almost walked pass her but for some strange reason, I turned back and approached her. I said to her "excuse me this is going to sound really weird, but do you have a bible", she responded by saying "yes, you are lucky we have only one more left". It felt as though God had reserved that one bible for me-there it was, my confirmation about my experience from God. Throughout the rest of the few weeks left of university, I read the bible but most of the time it made no sense to me, it felt that most scriptures were metaphorical which caused me to quickly loose interest. I carried on praying and took a hard look at my life, there were some obvious sins I was still committing, so I decided to let them go. I didn't know what this new journey of mine was going to be like, but it was fresh and gave me a new perspective about God that I was open to explore.

CHAPTER 15

The True Reality about Adulting

House sharing with others seemed like the better option when searching for places to live, if I was to save money to support my future. When mum found that I had been offered a job half an hour's drive away from the house, she automatically assumed that I will be moving back home then commute to work.

When I explained to her that this was not my plan, she seemed confused and didn't understand why this was the case. I didn't tell her my reason (which was due to all the things we had gone through for many years and that I was simply avoiding further conflict) however she may have sensed this.

My reluctance to move back home caused us some minor conflict, in which my aunt got involved with. She sided with mum and their argument was that the money used for renting elsewhere could support mum and my sisters, and that it made no sense for me to pay so much money when I can drive and get to work in 30minutes. I finally gave in and decided to consider what they were saying, I felt a bit guilty about wasting money that could support mum and my sisters however, what pushed me to agree was the realisation of my working hours limiting my time at home. The conclusion to my analysis after having a good, hard think about the living situation. I planned for most weekends to be spent out of the family home, with this in mind I decided to move back home. In July 2015, I graduated with a degree in social work, it was a great feeling, one I will never forget.

Just over two years of employment in my now 3rd post graduate role, I quickly discovered that the dreams I had been sold about life beginning after university was false! In fact, the truth is, there was no life after university. The reality was that I spent soo much time commuting to work and although the actual work fluctuated between the average eight hours (but sometimes more due to the nature of my job), commuting time combined was overall 11 hours a day.

It was too early to do anything before work when I woke up and too late to do anything afterwards. Often by the time I got home, I was so tired that my only option was to sleep in order to get enough energy to do the same thing the following day, and the day after. My weekends consisted of catching up with work at home in order to ensure that I was able to manage my caseload the following week.

I first started working in a children's home, followed by multiple teams in children's social care. The more I worked, the more I started to feel sorry for myself. I eventually got to the point, where I felt overwhelmed and was considering another career path. I had to find hope and some reassurance that there was more to life, than just a life of work. This is when I began to feel the full effect of finding my purpose in life with, the help of God. The questions I had asked myself when at university, about whether there was more to life, was now more prevalent than ever and I was in desperate need to find the answer.

Driving through early morning and evening rush hour traffic, was when I noticed how programmed people have become. The site of many people dressed in suits stuck in their cars with the lifeless look on their faces, motivated me even more to get out of the system I sometimes felt entrapped in. I kept saying to myself, I refuse to be one of these older people sat in traffic doing a job that isn't fulfilling, working tirelessly chasing money but never having the time to spend it.

As days and weeks went past, I became more observant of the systems of work and I began to feel sorry for the older people I saw in cars during rush hours and the ones I saw at work too, some looked like they had given up on life. They looked like they had no energy left, but programmed and robotic with every moment, doing the same routine daily. I began to feel sorry for the mothers who had left their children in the care of others to raise them in order to work in a place where their time and skills were not valued. I began to feel sorry for the elderly people I saw who should have been retired resting on a sunny beach but worked because society, determined the suitable time for them to retire. Mothers, fathers, grandparents were all working but for what? Money? Confidence in their skills? Recognition of their hard work? At the expense of what? Their freedom?

These thoughts occupied my mind daily, before, during and after work. I began to question if others thought like I did. I mean did the people I saw, day in and day out, at work and in their cars during rush hour, know there was more to life? Had they noticed the systems of the world, the way I had? Are they trying to find a way out of it like me or had they just given up?

I concluded that societal systems were not designed for the benefit of mankind but rather to control them discreetly. From the education system through to the employment system. The truth is that we are trained from a young age to work for others never for others to work for us or to work for ourselves. The higher you go in your career the more money you get and the less time you have to spend it. The lower you stay in your career the less money you have and the more time you have to reminisce about how much you don't have and how you should be doing more. Fortunately, a few people in society had this revelation and had overcome the systems of the world (Martin L King Jr, Bill Gates, Akala and Suli Breaks), this gave me hope that it was possible to overcome it too although, it would mean making sacrifices.

CHAPTER 16

God Knows My Name

The more I questioned life, the more I drew closer to God. I bought myself a study bible for deeper understanding about his word as I wanted to know his ideas and views about all the things I was thinking about.

Eventually, I began to have many encounters with God. I had dreams constantly, some good and some scary, I heard his voice audibly and through reading the bible and, had my questions answered by preachers on Gospel TV stations. I felt the presence of God and the presence of demons. I felt the peace and joy of God, I began to have a deeper revelation and understanding about the world and began to have a different perspective about life specifically my life. It felt as though my life was starting to make sense and everything that I had experienced in my life was for a purpose and a reason.

I finally had the full understanding that I was created for a purpose and that the unsettling feeling that I had experienced for so long was my spirit's way of telling me that I needed to start walking in line with my purpose. I understood that God had to isolate me to refine me, to renew my way of thinking, to help me recover my identity in him and most importantly to prove to me that he was real and knew my name, regardless of what I had believed in the past. I found comfort and excitement in coming home after work and praying and reading the bible for hours eager to see what revelation I would receive next. I felt excited about feeling God's presence and his peace in my bedroom.

I felt excited about the personal jokes I would share with God and the Holy Spirit. I remember thinking to myself that I am having more fun alone with God than I have ever had going out clubbing and partying. Although I had invites here and there from friends to go out, I politely turned this down. It was as though my interest and focus had changed. I didn't like the same things my old self liked. I was a new person in Christ and rediscovering my lost identity.

CHAPTER 17

The Process of Restoration

Although excited about this new lifestyle, I was still a bit shy to speak boldly of the experiences with God which I encountered in my private space, simply because I knew I would sound senseless to most people. There were also two issues in my way, that I constantly asked God to help me with. One was the issue of lust and the other was unforgiveness in my heart towards mum and dad.

Although things had gotten better at home, there were still occasions where I and mum would argue. I didn't know what I wanted from her exactly or what I wanted her to acknowledge but I had expectations. Maybe I needed her to tell me that she believes me, to apologise for falsely accusing me of the many things all these years, to look at me differently, to look at me the way she did when I was younger?

I don't know what I wanted but I knew things were still unsaid and that bothered me. It bothered me because every time I thought of what I had gone through, my emotions would rise again. I would feel myself getting angry with a lot of resentment in my heart towards her. This was difficult for me because I was further in my walk with God and understood that I needed a clean heart and needed to forgive just like how God had forgiven me for all my sins through the death of his son Jesus. I just didn't know how to, I think I tried physically but not emotionally and spiritually. Often, things were fine, and it seemed as though I had forgiven until something triggered, and then it all came rushing back.

The unforgiveness in my heart entrapped me, I felt like a bird trapped in a cage looking out at its reflection thinking about what it would be like to fly and be free whilst holding the key to the cage in its mouth. Just like the caged bird I felt trapped by unforgiveness, I sometimes wondered what it would be like to be free from the cage of the resentment, anger and the ill feelings I felt towards mum and dad. Just like the caged bird I had the key (forgiveness) to set myself free but often looked at the possibility of freedom from unforgiveness, instead of freeing myself.

It is often said that unforgiveness is like "drinking poison and hoping the other person dies". I felt first-hand what the true meaning of this statement meant, the sad reality is that I don't think mum even knew I was still holding on to the hurt she had caused me all these years. By now it had been about 5 years. Throughout this journey with God, I had located myself two spots near my house where I often drove to for a chat with God, for hours when I couldn't hold in my emotions. Sometimes I would go there to cry, other times to read my bible, pray or to have a nap away from home. My car became my second home, a place where I felt comfortable and at peace with. An argument with mum on one of my days at home is what led me to drive to one of the spots I had located near my house. I don't remember the specific details of the argument, but it was about an accusation which caused me to feel extremely upset. I parked up and began to cry out to God until I had no more tears to share. I could feel that my eyes had swollen, and my head was beginning to hurt.

I asked God about what to do as I no longer wanted to live at home, I became frustrated at the fact that I had a choice to leave home (without any implications) yet exercised patience to remain despite everything I was going through. I began to assess the different options I had concerning how I would move and where to. In this moment, I heard a small still voice say to me "go back home and tell your mum you forgive her". I wasn't sure if what I heard was what I heard, so I checked again with God and questioned if he was sure as I thought that I had already forgiven her. I heard the voice again say, "go back home and tell your mum you forgive her". I stayed put for a while and began to contemplate whether to follow the advice of the still voice or not.

I was mature enough in my faith to know the voice of God so there was no doubt that it was his instruction. I personally didn't feel that the instruction was correct. After some time, I decided to go ahead with the instruction given as I didn't want to consciously disobey God, simply because I knew his ways are always right and perfect even if we (his children) do not understand them.

Of course, things never plan out in the way we always imagine them in our heads. When I went back home and said to mum that "I forgive you". She retaliated straight away by inquiring about what she has done to need my forgiveness. Mum didn't seem to understand what she needed forgiveness for, and to be honest I didn't understand why God asked me to say that to her as a part of me knew how the conversation would turn out and the other part thought that I had already forgiven her.

I mean, it didn't make sense for me to be mature in my walk with God and still hold onto unforgiveness. Afterall I was saved, I prayed daily and was having numerous encounters with God. If I hadn't forgiven her then how did I get this far in my walk with God, considering how much he commands us to forgive others in his word.

I don't remember if the conversation ended well that night or not, but it led to mum and I having another conversation about the same issue on a different day. This time mum was sat outside in our garden and called me over for a chat. As we were going back and forth about our perspectives about the accusations and the impact it has had on the both of us, mum at some point said "I believe you". The moment those words came out of her mouth, it felt as though a huge weight had been lifted off me. I felt free as a bird. I felt as though I could fly out of a cage that I had been trapped in for so long.

Those three words "I believe you" made me realise something that day. The words made me realise that, I had allowed the unforgiveness to hold me hostage. I looked at mum and I said to her "that's all I needed to hear", as I spoke those words tears started to flow down from my face. The tears in my eyes were saying I had to learn to be dependent on myself emotionally for five years. I have held resentment in my heart. I have cried myself to sleep. I have felt judged by you. I have lost my best friend and role model. I have lost my mum and now, I feel drained. The little girl who was overjoyed to see her mum for the first time at the age of 11 could no longer recognise her mum. Mum proceeded to explain that she wasn't there for me because she had to be there for herself and that she was affected too. Although part of me understood her I don't know if I agreed with it. This is because there was no basis for the accusation and as a child, I had lost my emotional

emotional dependency, leaving me feeling, vulnerable, isolated and emotionally burdened a very heavy weight for any young person to carry.

When I was younger, I used to get upset when people commented that I didn't resemble my mum due to my desperation to be just like her. Mum was perfect in my eyes. She made no mistakes, she was always right, she was my superhero and meant everything to me. To have that taken away from instantly and for a long period of time left me feeling lost and emotional unstable.

At times I felt that mum was in battling with herself, because she was meant to love me like a mother would, however, at times it felt like I was her enemy. This confused me because that was my first reality check concerning my relationship with mum since I moved to the UK to join her in 2004. This reality check killed my naivety about the term "perfect". There is no such thing as a perfect relationship or a perfect person. Mum was human, she made mistakes just like you and I, she misinterpreted things that were said, she tried to defend herself where she thought she had to and at times struggled to take responsibility for her actions in cases where she got it wrong. This reality though struggled to sink into my mind because my expectations about my relationship with mum were exceeded until things turned around.

Although I was trying to process this new perception of mum, a huge part of me was also trying to desperately hold onto the old perception of mum I had admired so greatly, a hopeful yet despairing balance.

Those words mum uttered to some extent set me free, I could breathe and take in the air again, I could somewhat be myself again but the residue and damaged caused over the years is something I am still dealing with. The huge residue of mistrust was and still is something I am working on to date. Even now as an adult I sometimes catch myself feeling a need to explain myself all the time due to the fear of not being believed.

My Reflective Account about Confession

I believe everyone will experience a moment in their life whereby their superhero is no longer that, but human just like you and me. Your case of unforgiveness may be completely different to mine. Maybe you have been hurt by a partner, a friend, a colleague, a teacher or someone you trusted. Maybe you also have experienced an incident that turned your life upside down or caused you some emotional distress, physical and/ or psychological damage. Maybe you were abused as a child or have resentment toward an absent father, maybe your heart has been broken by someone you loved dearly, or you have been betrayed by someone you called a friend.

Whatever the case might be, I know that it may have caused some damage that has stayed with you for weeks, months and maybe years. Maybe you think you have forgiven the person (s) who has hurt you but are somehow still affected every time you see them, hear their name or think about what they have put you through.

Just like me, I thought that I had forgiven mum until God confronted me about approaching her and confessing that I have forgiven her. The revelation I now have about why confession is important can be summed up in two points. One, the act of confession with your mouth has a lot of power.

Although, you may have said in your head that you have forgiven, something happens spiritually when you say it out loud. Confessing this out loud to the person (if available or appropriate) is one way of starting the recovery process.

When you confess to the person that you forgive them, it becomes reality. There is a reason why the bible warns us about being careful with what we say. Your words have power! You can speak the change you want to become (either negatively or positively) into the atmosphere. God created the world through his words, "let there be light, and there was light", he created the entire universe through his words- therefore we cannot underestimate the power in confession of forgiveness. In cases where it might be inappropriate to talk to your offender, I recommend that you still confess that you forgive the person during prayer time with God.

Hearing yourself speak those words reaffirms your faith because we say out loud what we believe in and what we have faith in. This leads me into my second point about confession. Have you heard of any cases whereby people's self-esteem has been destroyed based on the words spoken over them continuously by a parent, teacher, guardian or boyfriend/girlfriend. Or maybe have found yourself speaking and acting like a person you spend a lot of time with? Well, we become by- products of our environments and begin to believe what we hear repeated to us over and over again. The bible talks about how faith comes by hearing the word of God. This simply means that we begin to have faith and believe in what we hear overtime.

When you hear yourself say "I forgive you" you start to believe it and start to live the confession you make. You may need to make this confession more than once, it may be something you have to do daily, it may hurt to hear yourself speak it out loud and may cause you some distress but push through and I guarantee that you will get to a place whereby you can speak openly about your struggle without offence, resentment or hurt. This is the place you should desire to be, this is a good place to be.

CHAPTER 18

My Lonely Battle with Lust

Lust was an issue I constantly prayed to God about due to the frustration it caused me. I had made huge progress and had completely stopped watching porn alongside cutting down masturbation but not entirely. I felt guilty and would beat myself up about it, every time I messed up. I knew it was wrong and even though, had cut down significantly, I was beginning to feel lonely as time went on during my isolation process with God. It had almost been a year since I was saved. I loved being in God's company but sometimes, missed having physical comfort.

Every time I felt alone, I was quick to remind God about the deal we made at the beginning of the year. Our deal for a husband (the next guy I met) in exchange for all my attention and dedication to him, his word and plan for my life for one year. I often reflected on the list I made for what I wanted in a husband and imagined what he would look like, sound like, smell like, dress like and even feel like.

Sex wasn't an option for me anymore until marriage which is why, number one agenda on my husband's list, was a man who was closer to God than I was so that the conversation about sex wouldn't even be up for discussion. Though excited about the husband God had for me, I couldn't ignore the physical manifestations of my frustration with lust. I just wanted a physical hug sometimes.

God had transformed my views about marriage entirely and marriage became something I deeply desired but this time for the long run. I had spent one month studying about godly relationships, the role of a wife and the role of husband and I was finally seeing men in the way God intended, as head of a home, to be respected and valued, to be cherished and supported, to be leaders and protectors. I had even tested myself on how I would be as a wife and showed God that I would be faithful and value marriage in the way he commands when he finally brought me my man. I made no effort to seek for my future husband as I knew the man was supposed to find me, I just had to make sure I was prepared to receive him when he finally came.

When I made the deal with God, I was specific with what I wanted and how I wanted it. I didn't want to go through the dating system again to fish him out as I didn't want to go back on the progress made as a child of Christ. I had come too far in my walk with God to make certain mistakes, I was now aware of God's standards and in fact feared messing up the relationship I had built with him. Days, weeks and months went by and the feeling of being alone grew stronger and stronger. The frustration was what led me to entertain Jordan when he contacted me. It had been months since we last spoke, the last contact we had was just before I finished university whereby, he talked about his plans to flee to Nigeria, following a car accident caused by him. He told me that he was planning on going to Nigeria because he was driving without a licence and caused an accident which will likely send him back to prison, as he was still on probation.

When he called me, he told me that he was in the UK temporarily to make some money and then would go back home where he was starting a new life. He said that his plan was to set up a studio in Nigeria and sounded passionate about this. I was excited for him because music is something, he was good at and it sounded as though he was starting to settle and do things the right way.

During our conversations over days, I shared parts of my new journey with God with him and he also shared with me that he was planning on attending church and was taking God seriously. He mentioned that he would like to see me before he left. Although hesitant to begin with, I agreed to it because I was feeling alone, and he came at the right time. The feeling of loneliness combined with his physical touch led my mind to wonder into things I knew would be displeasing to God. I tried so hard to resist but failed and we ended up sleeping together when we met. I was extremely disappointed in myself and I think he knew that based on my silence throughout the rest of our time together. I was disappointed in myself because I was due to celebrate my 1st year anniversary of being celibate in a couple of days and that was ruined in an instant due to lack of self-control. He wasn't to blame, I was.

I was so disappointed in myself and at the prospect that God was disappointed in me too that, I avoided talking to God about it. I didn't want God to judge me, I didn't want him to condemn me and I didn't want to revisit the moment with him again due to the guilt I felt. I struggled to pray because I felt like a hypocrite, I didn't think that God would listen to my prayers, until I addressed it with him and that was something, I simply wasn't ready to do due to the guilt I felt.

This guilt is what caused me to change my telephone number to block further contact from Jordan. It was the first thing I did during a morning break from work. Following on from this, I received messages from him on skype stating that he was unable to contact me despite his attempts. I plucked up the courage to send him a message explaining why I had changed my number. I was serious about God and I felt that my association with him will pull me back. I had come too far in my walk with God to just dabble around sin. I apologised and then blocked him because I had concluded that my walk with God was more important to me than the bond we had built over the years. When I eventually spoke to God, the overwhelming feeling of his love for me caused me to realise that he wasn't only my God but also my father. I expected judgement, I expected condemnation, I expected rejection but instead I received love. A love so powerfully overwhelming I still feel the raw emotions (I did then) when I think about it to date.

I took this opportunity to block and delete the numbers of people in my life whom I felt did not and would not play a significant role to help me with my walk with God. This act to me was my confirmation about how serious I was concerning my walk with God but more significantly this act was the beginning of the breaking of soul ties.

Jordan played a significant role in my life especially in my dark seasons. Even though I was fully aware that he was not the guy for me, I was afraid to let him go because I had subconsciously associated him with the feeling of safety. I was afraid to let him go because he was my escape when things were bad at home. I was only able to let go of him when I found a new safety-net in God.

My Reflective Account about the Trap of Loneliness

The feeling of being alone can sometimes corrupt our judgement and cause us to make decisions we might regret later. Just like feeding your physical body when you get hungry, feeling alone is your body's' way of telling you that it needs to be fed with social contact.

Being alone is not the same as feeling lonely, you can be alone and still feel satisfied if you are comfortable with your own company. On the other hand, you can be in a crowd of people and feel lonely. Being alone is temporary and can be resolved through some interventions. Although not a mental health issue, loneliness has close links with mental and emotional wellbeing. It is important to identify the difference between the two as they intertwine with each other but mean different things.

During my season of feeling alone, I sometimes interpreted this feeling as loneliness which amplified my feelings at the time leading to frustrations great enough to cause me to stumble in my journey with God. If I had reflected on why I felt alone, it is possible that my actions to solve this would have been different. I was very comfortable with my own company (maybe too much leading to the feeling of being alone) and preferred this over socialising at times. Although I learnt a lot within this time about myself, socialising with others or finding ways to distract my mind at times would have been a useful intervention to the feeling of being alone.

Physical suggestions to help combat the feeling of being alone include: Joining the gym or a club of interest, attending social events taking place in your local area, meeting friends for lunch or dinner, getting involved with charitable work within local areas, visiting elderly care homes to volunteer or becoming a befriender (loneliness is a prevalent issue among the elderly within the community due to losses associated with age). These are just a few ideas of what you can get involved in, if you are beginning to feel alone. Unattended feelings of being alone could lead into loneliness, don't allow yourself to fall into the same trap I did. Keep yourself and your mind occupied. An occupied mind leaves little room for distraction.

In line with the physical suggestions above, the spiritual elements of the feeling of being alone cannot be dismissed. I don't know about you, but I found out that when I felt alone, my mind started to wonder into thoughts I shouldn't have entertained. The devil has likes to whisper things to us when our minds are not filled and open to distraction. The bible talks a lot about the feeling of being alone and the feeling of loneliness, in fact there are many comforting scriptures in the bible about the feeling of being alone and loneliness (Psalm 27:10, 1 Samuel 2:22, Psalm 25:16, 1 Peter 5:7). Jesus felt lonely at some point during his ministry, he was betrayed, he was misunderstood and on the cross he said, "My God, my God, why have you forsaken me?"

Despite how we may be feeling, we need to understand that God is a God of relationships, it is his nature, he is a trinity and clearly likes the idea of communing with others. Examples can be found in the Book of Genesis after God's creation of man. God said, "it is not good for man to be alone, I will make a helper suitable for him". God knows about what it feels like to be alone and lonely, although it may seem as though you are alone, he is with you, he sees you, he hears your cry for help, he knows the suffering in your heart. He is more than able to help you if you allow him to.

Just like the physical suggestions above, there are spiritual suggestions that can help you when feeling alone. Worship and praise in lonely seasons will uplift your spirit. Praise and worship will help you develop an eternal perspective on your situation. It reminds you of what God can do and what he has done for you. It pushes your worries into the background, it fosters an awareness of God's presence and will open your heart up to receive God's glory. Fellowship with other believers in your lonely season as this will encourage you. The unity and experiences of oneness with other true believers can be a starting point to ending the feeling of being alone.

Feeding your mind with the word of God (either through watching sermons online or reading the bible) prepares you and gives you the tools to fight the whispers of the enemy in your lonely season. Remember that you are not alone. God is always with you. You may not be hearing him because your mind can be a battle ground and the other voices are too loud. The voice of the lord is gentle. Seek out for his voice and take practical steps (listed above both physically and spiritually) to help you overcome your season of loneliness.

CHAPTER 19

A Tender Heart

As part of God's transformation in changing my perspective about men, I couldn't escape his attempts to change my mind-set about my father. At times when I prayed, I heard the still small voice saying pray for your father. This voice became so regular that I began to pray for him without hearing the voices' instructions.

With time, my heart grew tender towards dad and my hardened heart softened towards him. I began to pray for the lord to keep and guide him and began to think that maybe there is a reason why he wasn't there for me as much as I would have liked him to be. I was looking forward to the time when we rekindle our relationship so much so that I asked God for a wish; to have my father walk me down the aisle on my wedding day one day, this wish was made in 2016.

Although this may seem trivial, as that is a normal tradition with most weddings, my case was a bit different. My case was different in the sense that for this to happen, mum and dad would have to communicate and come into an agreement and the thought of it seemed impossible. However,

I was willing to test God as I had dedicated over a year of my life to him (and had positive experience with him) and had faith that it would come to pass. Although I had no knowledge of how it would happen, I knew God's ways are not mine and had no business questioning how it would happen.

I began to pray about it. My telephone contact with dad increased a bit over time. I had some questions to ask dad when we finally had the opportunity to meet and sit down properly. My intentions of asking the question when the opportunity came was not to cause distress or guilt, I just wanted to hear his side of the story and see what can be done to repair the years lost. I wasn't anxious about the response I could get from him, as I had already forgiven him in my heart. I was open and willing to build and embrace a relationship with him despite the years lost.

CHAPTER 20

The 'Real Me'

Eventually God began to reveal to me part of my life's assignment. God kindly dropped an idea in my imagination to set up an organisation that will raise awareness about cultural practices affecting people from Black and Minority Ethnic communities using research and training. The journey to and from work didn't seem as bad anymore. When stuck in traffic, I used that opportunity to plan the next move concerning the idea God had given me. I came to realise that time is precious and had to be use wisely. I didn't always need a pen and paper or to be sat down in a quiet place to plan things. My mind became my pen and paper.

From the moment I sat in my car in the morning, to the moment I sat back in the car on my way home and even during break times, my mind was constantly planning how I was going to make this idea a reality. This idea gave me (and is still giving me) the mental freedom I needed to keep me stable in the systems of the world until God's bigger plan is revealed.

The more I thought about it and done some research the bigger the vision became. The frustrations I faced at work turned into motivation towards the idea. I became excited about my future and was ready to invest and put in the time and work required to bring the vision to life. I shared this idea with a few friends but mostly kept it between myself and God. The idea is now a successful platform known as The Ideal Culture Standard (TICS).

Though my daily routine and my life hadn't changed, my perspective about life in general had and this is a transformation that I still get excited about daily. The bible talks about how "we do not wrestle with flesh and blood but against principalities, against powers, against the rulers of the darkness of this world", God revealed to me that majority of the spiritual and mental battles we face daily are battles of the mind. The principalities he refers to are principles we have built in our minds over years based on negative experiences we may have encountered. These principles built over years, some general, core beliefs and values are not easily broken.

These principles in a form of a tower represent the tainted mind, heart and spirit. Each brick to the tower represents unforgiveness, low self-esteem, abuse, domestic violence, neglect, assault, a broken heart and any experience you may have had that has shaped your identity. A representation of a damaged tower one, that needs to be broken down but not harshly or aggressively due to the harmful impact it could cause but chipped away brick by brick to ensure little to no damage or residue. This is the work God was doing in me, ever so gentle and nurturing in order to renew me, my identity and my mind. I can share my story with you because some parts of the bricks have been chipped and renewed. I have found a new identity in Christ and I love it. The ability to see the world around me through God's eyes alone gives me so much joy and peace, a spiritual gift that can be obtained only from God.

Want to know how my story ends?

I am still pioneering on with the vision of the organisation God planted in my imagination, but this time jointly with my husband. God is still revealing more of his purpose and plans for my life to me, one being sharing my testimonies and lessons through books just like this one.

I met my now, precious husband approximately a year after I made my deal with God whom God used to help chip away some more bricks to build up new ones. We got married a little over 2 years of being together in September 2018 and my father walked me down the aisle just as I had wished for in 2016 and our relationship is still going strong.

I am totally and completely healed from unforgiveness and my relationship with mum was restored to its original state but was later strained during my journey to the alter. However, this time I had the experience about the importance of forgiveness to get me through this second test smoothly and quickly, with results of freedom and peace.

Who knows, I might share my testimony and the lessons learnt from the second test in another book but for now I want to talk you through the four main lessons I learnt throughout my journey. These lessons are ones I believe you should know about if you are dealing with unforgiveness in your heart or are going through a testing time in your life.

LESSONS LEARNT

Lesson One

Forgiveness is An Act of Strength Not Weakness

Forgiveness is often something we are told to do, especially if growing up in a Christian home. Forgive as God has commanded, forgive because he has forgiven you, but what does it really mean to forgive. Does forgiveness means forgetting too? It is easy to forgive people if the offence caused is minor, but how do you truly forgive when the person you are dependent on, the person you love dearly accuses you of something that turns your life upside down? How do you forgive when you are made to feel like an outcast? How do you forgive when you are so deeply hurt that you struggle to trust?

Forgiveness is not as easy as it is often portrayed, in my case it took me years of my life to let go of pain, hurt and disappointment. I know what it feels like to have your day ruined by a single thought of your offender and I know what it feels like to be free from emotional bondage. It is not easy to forgive people who deeply hurt you, as forgiveness can sometimes feel as though you are allowing the offender to get away with the offence, they caused you, seeming as tough, you are weak and easily taken advantage off. However, one thing I learnt in the years of unforgiveness is that, unforgiveness in the heart leads to a lot of other things. Unforgiveness in the heart has power to change your personality, it has power to corrupt your day, it has power to keep you up at night and It has power to control your life. It controls you like a puppet. It's a thief of joy and peace but the source of anger and bitterness. Unforgiveness gives the enemy legal rights to access other areas in your life.

Unforgiveness can damage your health. Recurring or chronic anger has an impact on blood pressure, heart rate and immune response. The constant changes in the body increases the risk of anxiety, depression, diabetes, heart disease and many more conditions. Unforgiveness in your heart slowly kills your mood, it slowly kills your personality, it slowly kills your optimism, and slowly kills your heart, eventually leading to emotional and spiritual death.

There is power in forgiveness, there is freedom in forgiveness. We often see forgiveness as a favour unto the person (s) who has hurt us, but the truth is that it is a favour unto ourselves. When you forgive others, you favour yourself because you are not allowing yourself to suffer the consequences of someone else's actions. Forgiveness is not an expression of weakness but rather an expression of power.

Forgiveness is saying that I love myself enough to not let other people's actions control me. This speaks power and strength in a person's ability to take charge over their own mind and emotions. It is often said that it takes twenty-one days to form or break a habit. I have tested this theory many times in my life and have both succeeded and failed.

One thing I have learnt though, is that habits when not broken become grounded and rooted, when grounded and rooted becomes second nature, when it becomes second nature, it becomes principle. A principle can be defined as a "fundamental truth or proposition that serves as the foundation for a system of belief or behaviour or for a chain of reasoning". Principles are the foundation of beliefs and beliefs have an influence on one's mind which has power to control one's actions. The mind is, if not the most important, one of the most important tools we possess, although controls our actions, it can be easily controlled and influenced. What I hadn't realised is that I had allowed the unforgiveness in my heart to turn into a principle.

I used to question God about why unforgiveness ruled me for so long. His response to me was, that I allowed it to happen so that you would understand the significance forgiveness. This revelation and understanding about the importance of forgiveness is what got me through another significant event later down in life and will get me through many future tests. God was preparing me for the next season in my life.

It is important to know that forgiveness does not mean forgetting, you can forgive and not forget if what you remember is not used as a tool to take you back into the place of darkness. I still remember what I went through but when I think about it, I am no longer bitter but rather grateful to have come out of the dark place. I am grateful to be able to share my testimony to help you and most importantly, grateful that my remembrance of events is a constant reminder about the importance of forgiveness. Forgiving those who have hurt you requires you to be intentional and requires you to take some practical steps. Below are four (4) steps I took to help me heal:

1) Pray for the person who has offended you: Praying for anyone requires compassion, empathy and faith in the fact that God will answer your prayers on their behalf. Therefore, it is impossible to pray for someone and resent them at the same time. During my testing time with mum, after I was saved, I often prayed for her. I prayed for God to bless her, favour her, give her what her heart desires and help her forgive whoever has offended her, so that she can be set free as I now

knew what freedom was and what bondage (as consequences of other peoples' actions) felt like also.

The bible talks about loving your enemies and praying for those who persecute you. Why is this? Why does God command us to bless those who curse us and love those who abuse us? The simple reason is that prayer is a spiritual tool that can be used to deal with physical problems. When you pray for your offenders something takes place spiritually which has an impact on the physical realm. When you pray for your offenders, overtime your hardened heart softens and you begin to genuinely care for your offender. This genuine care often causes a change of perspective and heart towards the offender.

This fresh perspective is what promotes positive actions and responses to them, even if their actions towards you are not always positive. Through positive actions, Gods love is shown to the offender. God's love is unconditional. It is without conditions unlike human love. It is sacrificial and always wins. The resentment you may have towards a person, begins to disintegrate when you pray for them.

Prayer is a leading pastime in gratitude and reflection, prayer amplifies God's goodness in our lives and weakens our views about the small things in life taking dominion over us. An improved attitude, better sense of self, forgiveness, hope, freedom and a positive outlook on life are some of the benefits of prayer.

2) Be conscious of your thoughts and speak positivity: It is not uncommon to have negative thoughts about people who have offended you even after you have forgiven them. Sometimes, past hurt creeps up and triggers can spring up negative thoughts that, if not regulated can quickly take you back to the place of darkness and hate. Therefore it is important to be conscious of your thoughts and to correct them immediately, if you find yourself regressing.

Being conscious of your thoughts although very vital, sometimes is not enough. You must also speak positively about the offender and/ or yourself when you find yourself drifting. The affirmation of positive words over your thoughts play a key role when forgiving past hurt. Saying things like, "I have forgiven [insert offenders name]", "I am no longer holding hate in my heart", "I am free from resentment", "I am strong", "I am created in Gods image so I am of love" and "I will not allow my thoughts to control me" can help during the times of regression.

As mentioned in one of my reflective accounts above, the bible makes it very clear that we have power in our tongue and to be careful with what we say as our words have life. You cannot underestimate the power of your words. The world was created because, God spoke it into existence, that is how powerful words are! When having negative thoughts about your offender, speak the change you want to see.

3) Understand that forgiveness is for your benefit and not for the benefit of your offender: When you grasp this concept, you will be quick to forgive when people hurt you. I am urging you to make yourself understand this not only because it makes things easier but also because it is the truth. Forgiveness means that you have made peace with the hurt and are

ready to move on. If you have held a grudge or hold unforgiveness in your heart you know that it takes a lot of energy and time and can be very draining both physically and emotionally. Forgiveness frees up a lot of space in your mind to think about other things which may be of interest to you. When you forgive, you sleep better at night as you are not kept awake thinking about the hurt and pain, you are happier in yourself because you are not held back by mental bondage.

Forgiveness is for your benefit. This is why God commands this of us, his intention isn't to supress our emotions but, to free us from the damaging ones. Aside from the biblical aspect of forgiveness, psychology also shows that benefits of forgiveness include reduced anger, hurt, depression, stress and increases the feeling of optimism, hope, compassion, and emotional and spiritual growth.

4) Be proud of yourself: Sometimes we can be a bit hard on ourselves when we reflect on past experiences and realise how long it took for us to forgive others and how long it took to move on. This realisation comes after we have the full understanding of how forgive-

ness benefits us. It can feel like you've wasted so much time and could have been freed much sooner. This feeling can cause some upset if pondered on for long periods of time. If you are at this stage, forgive yourself. Don't waste more time thinking about what you should have done. The chances are things happened the way they were meant to happen. There is a reason it took you this amount of time, this reason might not be revealed to you until later on in life, so don't beat yourself up about it. I have only recently realised that, it took five years of my life to forgive because that is how long I needed to understand the significance of it. Anything less wouldn't have communicated its significance so powerfully.

The length of time and energy it cost me, is what led me to say that "I will never allow any offence to affect me for that long ever again in my life" and mean it wholeheartedly. The length of time and energy it cost me, is what has wired up my mind to forgive even before an offence occurs.

Lesson Two

The Soul Ties We Build in Testing Seasons

Be mindful about who you associate yourself with in testing times as this can have an overwhelming influence over all areas of your life. Meeting Jordan during my testing time at home with mum, shaped the type of relationships I attracted throughout many years of my life until I got saved. Although he was not aware that he was my escape, I was, and this awareness became embedded into my subconscious mind.

The subconscious mind is an unquestioning servant that works day and night to make your behaviour fit a pattern consistent with your emotionalised thoughts. The subconscious mind tends to be overlooked. We tend to focus more on the conscious mind however, the subconscious mind is a part of our mind that notices and remembers information when we are not actively trying to do so. It influences our behaviour even though we may not realise this. It has a lot of power and greatly influences our conscious minds.

Due to my conscious awareness that Jordan was my escape, I built a very strong emotional connection to him. Jordan was in my eyes more than what he should have been, simply because I saw him as a part of the solution to my problem. This association of him, clouded my judgement despite the fact that we were not compatible for each other, based on the future I wanted for myself.

The soul tie I built with him subconsciously reminded me that he was a protector and an escape in times of needs, my security and my safety. This subconscious reminder is what kept me in need of him despite, my conscious awareness that we were not meant for each other. This subconscious reminder is what led to attracting men of that nature even when I made conscious efforts not to. I had associated men like him to feeling safe and secure. The cycle of attracting men like him was something I questioned myself about although, at the time couldn't explain why. I now know that the reason for this was because of my soul tie with Jordan and a subconscious awareness of associating him with the feeling of safety.

You may have heard of the word soul tie, if you are of a faith. The term soul consists of your heart, will and emotions. The term tie can be defined as an attachment or bind to something or someone. Therefore, a soul tie is an attachment or bind to someone or something through the heart, emotions and ones will. This attachment is very strong due to the three components involved and is not easily broken. Your five (5) sense communicate to your soul. When you see, hear, touch, taste or smell something, you are communicating to your soul (mind and emotions) that you either like something or you don't, if you like something you are likely to submit your will to it.

In my case Jordan's looks, the words he spoke to me and how he felt communicated safety (I was distracted from my sorrows) to my mind and emotions, this then made me surrender my will to our connection as it didn't feel like I was in harm's way. This soul tie is what caused me to entertain him, even after salvation and clarity about what I wanted and needed in a man.

We must be careful with what we allow our souls to get tied to, when in testing seasons. Soul ties are not limited to people but can be to objects and experiences. Your soul can be tied to a specific place, items such as drugs and alcohol, and to experiences such as ones gained from misusing alcohol and drugs. Some people turn to drugs and alcohol when going through hardship, as an escape just like how Jordan was for me. This, then becomes an addiction, a soul tie that is very difficult to break.

Although, in difficult seasons we are often searching and yearning for peace and safety, at all times we must be conscious about soul ties. Fortunately for me, God found me and my soul became tied to his, so I was able to break my tie with Jordan because I found a new security and safety in God.

Lesson Three

"Do Not Air Your Dirty Laundry"

Talking to people about what we are going through can sometimes be very unsettling, especially if we do not know what their reaction will be towards us. We fear they might judge us, not believe us, disagree with us, laugh at us, belittle us or not be able to help us. Although this may be the case sometimes, it is not in majority of cases. Talking about what you are going through has many benefits:

- It helps you process what you're thinking.
- It could provide you with a solution, if the person you talk to has shared experiences
- It helps you see that you may not be alone in your thinking
- It helps you see things from various perspectives

Talking to a trusted person when struggling with problems helps you get a 360-degree view about the problem. At times when consumed with our own problems we amplify it, talking to someone about it relieves us a bit, especially when we no longer have the capacity to handle them all by ourselves.

Notice how I said a trusted person? This is very important because the person you talk to can either help and support you or make things worse for you. Talking to a friend of the offender will likely cause more harm than good as the friend will stay loyal and support the offender. Assuming the offender is a boyfriend or partner, talking to the offender's family about the offence is not wise as his family are more likely to support him.

Speak to someone who does not know you or your offender to minimise bias views. Someone without knowledge of you or the offender's history, someone without judgement, someone who wants the best for the both of you (recommendation of a professional counsellor or a minister at your place of worship).

I know it can seem very isolating when you feel like you have no one to talk to, isolation if not monitored can lead to depression which can have adverse consequences later down the line as explained in the first section of this book. No one knows what you are going through until you say something, no one knows how much you are hurting until you say it, and no one knows that you need help until you ask for it. Staying silent on issues affecting you can be dangerous, don't stay silent due to the fear of being judged by others. Don't stay silent because you think no one else can help you.

Don't stay silent because you are fearful of the consequences of speaking up or due to fear of increased conflict. Don't stay silent even if you haven't yet grasped what is happening to you, if you are hurting or if the idea of "do not air your laundry" is encouraged in your home. Just don't stay silent! I should have spoken to a counsellor at university when I had the opportunity to do so, do not make the same mistake I did, in thinking that I don't want to air my dirty laundry.

This statement is often taken out of context but even if it were in context the truth is that if the laundry is dirty, it needs to be cleaned and aired if not it stays wet and the bacteria stays in it (metaphorically speaking). Speaking about your pain and hurt is about seeking rehabilitation and restoration not airing dirty laundry. The true context of "airing dirty laundry" refers to issues that should be kept out of sight when people visit.

The context of "airing dirty laundry" is purely based around embarrassment and it is without an agenda. An example being a husband complaining amongst family friends by saying, "if my wife stops nagging so much, I might help more around the house". This statement has no agenda and its purpose is to clearly embarrass or cause some form of humiliation towards the wife in front of others. Talking to someone about your pain and hurt is far from an embarrassment to you or your offender because the agenda is to seek help and a solution to the problem. Subsequently, when you don't understand the context of this statement, you may be convinced that talking to someone about your hurt and pain is about discussing secrets in public.

"A problem shared is a problem halved" the meaning of this statement is that when you discuss your problems with a trusted person, it becomes easier to deal with. When you share your concerns with a trusted person, they are likely to do everything they can to help you overcome it often feeling as though they are carrying the burden with you.

Lesson Four

It Will All Make Sense

When we are going through things it is hard to see the outcome especially if what we are dealing with consumes our lives. Often, we become so consumed that we start to question why things happen to us. We may begin to bargain with God and may even loose hope when we do not get a response. During my testing time, my mind was very short sighted in its thinking because I was in survival mode. It wasn't until I came out that I realised that it was for a greater purpose. It did not make sense then, but it did when I overcame it.

I now understand that I had to go through the emotional heartache to understand forgiveness. I needed to understand the significance and importance of it. My understanding about the significance and importance of forgiveness in my teen years is what got me through my adult trials. I now understand that I had to go through what I did because it is part of my story, ministry and the assignment God has for my life.

I now understand that I had to go through the process to have a testimony. A testimony, in which I can help many people who may be holding onto unforgiveness in their hearts towards an absent father, a mother, an abuser, a friend, a manager, a partner or even towards themselves for something they may have done years ago. I now understand that I had to go through the trials in order to get the skills, education and experience to help me teach others who may be struggling. Everything you go through has a reason and a link to another area, aspect or season in your life. Now that I understand this concept, I am not discouraged by testing seasons. I see trials as opportunities to learn something that will benefit myself and others later in life. I encourage you to see things from this perspective for two (2) main reasons:

1) Because It makes things easier to deal with and shifts your focus in how you respond to trials and offenders

2) Because it helps you understand that your trials are just for a season, it will pass!

If I had known that my trial would become my testimony, help many people and that I would be writing a book about forgiveness eight years later, when I was going through my testing time, my response would have been different. I now know that I had to move back home for the forgiveness process to take place, I now know that I had to forgive my dad for our relationship to be restored as he would later play an unexpected and significant role in my life. I now know that the testing time in my teenage years was training me for adulthood tests. I now know that there is a reason for everything God permits us to go through. It may not make sense at the time, but it will when the season is over. Maybe I would have cried less and stressed less if I had known. I didn't know that it would all make sense, but you do, so use that to your advantage in your difficult seasons.

EXTRAS

A Prayer for Revelation and Strength to Forgive
A Prayer for Salvation
A Personal Note from Myself
Further Reading

A Prayer for Revelation and Strength to Forgive

Father, I am hurting, and I need your help. I have been hurt by [insert name] who I trusted and love. I want to forgive [insert name] but I don't know how. Father grant me the strength and grace to forgive them, for my heart is open to your guidance and leading, concerning this issue. I believe that you can help me love and cherish them again and I believe that you can heal me of the pain and hurt I am experiencing. I trust you and your word, and I believe that the blood of Jesus has restored me. Forgive me for not forgiving as you have asked, I am willing and open to try. Teach me, guide me, support me and comfort me.

In Jesus's name I pray Amen.

A Prayer for Salvation
(Romans 10:9-10, Ephesians 2:8-9, I John 1:9)

God, I am here before you today because I want to know you and build a relationship with you. I thank you for your son Jesus whom was sent to die for my sins so I can be one with you again. I believe that he is your son and I repent off my sins and ask that Jesus becomes the lord of my life. I ask for forgiveness and I ask that your spirit dwells in me and guides me from today forth. I ask for encounters with you today and pray for a deeper understanding about you and the plans and purpose you have for my life.

In Jesus's Name

Amen

Congratulations! Welcome to a new life in Christ, by faith you have received the lord as your personal saviour and now have his spirit (The Holy Spirit) living inside of you, speak to him, commune with him and he will guide your path. This journey that you are about to embark on with Christ will not be easy but certainly fulfilling and an adventure. Read the bible, find a bible based local church to fellowship with and enjoy your journey.

A Personal Note from Me

Hey

Just wanted to say thank you for taking the time out to read this book. I was so nervous to release this book because I did not know the type of response, I would get but here it is. I hope you enjoyed it and have learnt something from it. Please share with me if you found this book useful, you can send me an email on **ps-books@hotmail.com** I'd love to hear from you. You can also add me on Instagram - **ps.books** for updates about upcoming events and other books.

If you want to know more about "cultural" and silenced issues affecting Black and Minority Ethnic communities visit: **www.theidealculturestandard.org**. It is a free platform raising awareness about some of the issues I have addressed in this book through evidenced based articles. If you are a writer or have experienced some of these issues and would like to share your story you can write an article for our website. We are always encouraging people to share their experiences because this is how we raise awareness. You can write about a personal experience or write about a general experience, either way it will be beneficial. When you visit our website, click on the "write for us" page for more information about getting your work published on our website. If you have any questions to do with this platform send them to **info@theidealculturestandard.org**

Once again, thank you for your support it means a lot.

Love

Pam

Further Reading

All biblical scripture and quotes used were taken from the New International Version (NIV) Bible.

Hurt2Healing (2007-2019) *Scandal of the Absent Black Fathers in the UK*. UK: London. [13/02/2019]. Available at: http://hurt2healingmag.com/scandal-of-the-absent-black-fathers-in-the-uk/.

The Joh Hopkins University (n.d) *Forgiveness: Your Health Depends on It.* [11/03/2019]. Available at: https://www.hopkinsmedicine.org/health/healthy_aging/healt hy_connections/forgiveness-your-health-depends-on-it

Oxford University Press (2019) *Definition of principle in English: Principle.* UK. [13.02.2019] Available at: https://en.oxforddictionaries.com/definition/principle

Simple Psychology (2014) *Bobo Doll Experiment.* [13/02/2019]. Available at: https://www.simplypsychology.org/bobo-doll.html

Your Notes

What actions are you going to take to forgive the people who offend you?

Printed in Poland
by Amazon Fulfillment
Poland Sp. z o.o., Wrocław